# Toronto Interiors

# MODERN RESIDENTIAL DESIGN

Mhouse Inc.'s Warm Transitional project, and EM Design Studio's Private Residence (right).

# Toronto Interiors

CATHERINE MACINTOSH

FOREWORD BY PAOLO FERRARI

Figure.1
Vancouver/Toronto/Berkeley

25 26 27 28 29 5 4 3 2 1



Cataloguing data is available from Library and Archives Canada
ISBN 978-1-77327-265-8 (hbk.)

Design by Teresa Bubela
Editing by Linda Pruessen
Copy editing by Stephanie Fysh
Proofreading by Grace Yaginuma
Author photograph by Brett Elizabeth Photography

Front cover photograph by Scott Norsworthy
Back cover photograph by Valerie Wilcox Photography

Printed and bound in China by Shenzhen Reliance Printing Co., Ltd.

Figure 1 Publishing Inc.
Vancouver BC Canada
www.figure1publishing.com

Figure 1 Publishing is located in the traditional, unceded territory of the xʷməθkʷəy̓əm (Musqueam), Sḵwx̱wú7mesh (Squamish), and səlilwətaɬ (Tsleil-Waututh) peoples.

Mhouse Inc.'s Modern Minimalist project.

This book is dedicated to my son, Malcolm, my *raison d'être*; and to my one and only, Bruce.

Batay-Csorba Architects' High Park project.

# Contents



Wanda Ely Architect's
Palmerston project.

# Foreword

BY PAOLO FERRARI

THERE IS SOMETHING liberating about having a creative practice in a young city. I sometimes think of the weight that must be felt by creatives working in places that have long, deep-rooted histories, often impossible to ignore and incredibly imposing upon the artistic process. The more I've travelled, the more I have come to appreciate Toronto's newness and its ceaseless appetite to evolve.

This is a city informed by its diversity—a city that encourages an openness for ideas and new expressions. As such, the variety of design and architectural practices in Toronto is extremely rich. At once quintessentially Canadian and broadly global, the work you will find in *Toronto Interiors* is diverse in both philosophy and approach and moves effortlessly between what the city was and where it is going.

Toronto is a city where you have the space to dream.

Many of our friends and colleagues are represented here with commissions that present a vast range of aspirations. Residential projects often begin as a question of ritual and lifestyle. They are personal expressions and an intimate collaboration between creative and client. Though the homeowner is placed at the centre of decisions made, this type of work often requires great precision to push beyond the ask at hand. Imbuing these residences with poetry, rigour, and joy is where the creative act takes shape—celebrating the contrast between light and shadow, between neutrality and saturation, or between the qualities of built form and nature. All these considerations are innate to the creative process and require a sort of alchemy and an intuitive confidence to conceive.

Inspiration is a curious thing. It's not something easily acquired. It's a nebulous process of translating culture, context, need, and desire. It exists in the shadows and when uncovered, can be intoxicating. The work in this book is the result of a relentless dedication to the design process and the craft of building. For designers and architects, realizing these built works is not easy, but tremendously rewarding.

*Toronto Interiors* is an extraordinary achievement. I warmly invite you to take a journey through these pages and lose yourself within Toronto as it is, right *now*. I promise, a distinct and satisfying world full of boundless creativity and unique perspectives will reveal itself.

These Architects' House in the Hill project.

Leonardo da Vinci
HISTORY OF MODERN ART
RENDEZVOUS
ROTHKO

# Introduction

MY FASCINATION WITH houses and interior design has been with me most of my life. My favourite childhood pastime was rearranging a toy treehouse for squirrels with Beatrix Potter–style sitting rooms, table linens, and proper tea service. I recall listening intently as a child to my mother discussing her colour and fabric choices for our living room. She was studying interior design, and as I sat on the floor staring at her poster board assignment replete with tiny carpet samples and wallpaper swatches, I was mesmerized. It was like having a dollhouse that could be redone again and again. I flipped though wallpaper books imagining the castles or tiny closets that could be reborn if only for some paisley or toile. The room my mom designed, however, with its coral and green velvet and its bird-patterned upholstery, stayed with us for decades. In fact, when my mother eventually re-covered the sofa and chairs, those birds were right on point again. There were peacocks on the hallway walls, botanical vines and bright colours that spread out and up the staircase, bedspreads that matched the curtains. I loved it all.

Our house had every design magazine, and my sisters and I pored over them. When we went off to university, we were gifted with our own subscriptions. It's no wonder, then, that when I made my way into book publishing, and later magazines, I sent my résumé to *Canadian House & Home* magazine. It was a dream to be hired there. I interviewed top designers, wrote about incredible artists, and visited amazing spaces. From there, I continued my journey by writing and editing stories for local and international modern design magazines, websites, and books, but it was as editor-in-chief at *Designlines* that my admiration for our local talent really took hold. We have so many amazing artists, furniture makers, ceramicists, decorators, and architects right here in Canada.

When I met publisher Steve Cameron at the Interior Design Show a few years back, he had the most wonderful catalogue of books from Figure 1 on display—books on art, design, food, and Indigenous culture. We chatted about a love of books not just as tactile objects but, more importantly, as the record keepers of art and culture. When he asked me to write a book about the best Toronto interiors, focusing on studios that have made a mark on the city's design zeitgeist, I was thrilled to record a topic so near and dear to my heart. But how could I narrow it down? Countless designers collectively shape the look and feel of Toronto's homes. The studios selected for this

Kim Lambert Design's Annex project.

collection contribute to what is happening now, how the city's heritage homes are being restyled for how we live today, and how brave new architecture is redefining our streets.

Over the years I've spent as a magazine editor, thousands of photos of incredible houses have crossed my desk. I often have an immediate thought as to where the image hails from: white and bright from the west coast, natural and earthy from the east, urban and arty from Quebec, pitched-roof modern farmhouses from rural Ontario, and a vast range in between. Designers are influenced by their travels, their peers, the media, and, of course, the homes they are tasked with reinventing. For decades now, homeowners have had access to image banks, design publications, and fabrics and furniture that were once only "to the trade." All of this combines to create moments in time that define the city's architecture, interiors, fashion, and décor. But all things evolve and shift, including design. At one time, we all wanted big, open kitchens, and then we wanted walls again. Once we craved colour and pattern, and then spare and modern spaces—and back again. What's truly interesting is when design veers away from this sliding scale of trend and counter-trend, or "correction," as it were.

So, where are we now? In touring hundreds of spaces and speaking with the thirty studios featured in this book, a few topics have come up again and again. One of the most consistent refrains is that Toronto is not what it was a decade or two ago. Its distinct design direction has emerged thanks to the work of gifted professionals, including those profiled here, many of whom challenged the status quo long before the neighbours (and committee of adjustments) were ready. We seem to be trying to shake off a reputation for being safe and staid. The pandemic may have nudged this along by forcing us to look at our surroundings with a critical eye. Many of us spend much more time in our homes now than we did pre-pandemic, so it's no surprise, really, that we want those homes to reflect who we are and how we live. As the years have passed, the city has tried on a few outfits, grown up a lot, and altered its course several times, but it seems to be settling into an era—one defined by individuality and craftsmanship.

On the global stage, we've been playing catch-up with cities and countries that have more defined design languages—or rather, trying to find our footing as a city of many voices, many cultures, and many aesthetics. We love heritage, but we tear it down; we value high design, yet we don't embrace it fully. We are Canadian, after all, and a bit reserved, a bit self-deprecating. But Toronto the Good is shedding its beige attire and stepping out. Homeowners are taking risks—thinking not just of resale value but also about how they truly want to live, what starts their engines. Dare I say we are seemingly more passionate than we once were?

There are gems aplenty, and now, I think, Toronto has landed on its feet. It seems a perfect time to celebrate the amazing work done here. For decades, incredible architects and interior designers have been quietly

Lisa Lev Design's
Clarendon project.

ATWOOD
LEVINE
TORONTO

transforming private residences—ones I feel so lucky to have toured and photographed. I think a design tipping point has hit the streets in what is now the fourth-largest city in North America. Even so, it takes a certain amount of saturation and density for it to be felt by those coming to visit.

A friend from elsewhere once said to me, "Toronto—I don't get it." It's a fair thing to say. Toronto is a place you need to spend time in to understand. As one of the most diverse cities in the world, it defies pigeonholing. Our influences, not to mention our lived experiences, vary dramatically. Everyone's Toronto is different. The city is a veritable patchwork of cultures, styles, neighbourhoods, and languages. As City Hall defines it, we have 158 official neighbourhoods, and their streetscapes vary widely. Toronto is a place that needs exploring by bike, by foot, by transit. Doing so reveals the unique flavours and architecture of each enclave, big or small.

From the heritage rowhouses of Cabbagetown to the glass towers on the lake to the grand neo-Tudors in the Kingsway, bungalows in East York, and new builds in Forest Hill, there is indeed something for everyone. There's mid-century up in Don Mills and Victorian in the Annex—the styles are many and seemingly disconnected, but they inform our experiences here. Some, like our bay-and-gables, are distinctly Torontonian.

But what about the interiors? For decades, architectural styles have dictated interior floor plans and, in part, styles. Many of our 100- to 130-year-old homes have undergone renovations at some point or another, and most of what transpired in previous decades does not hold up now. It's no longer what we want. We don't live the way we did when these houses were built—we eat casually, we entertain differently, and we work at home.

Layered on top of these lifestyle changes are the demographic shifts that occur as each generation grows older. What your grandparents wanted does not always translate. Interiors are being completely overhauled—new staircases, room configurations, and walls—and decorated in ways that are wonderfully personal instead of following any particular era or trend. Like fashion, décor comes and goes, but timeless style reigns supreme, whether it's traditional, modern, or somewhere in between. Toronto homes vary dramatically in personal style: there are homes with colour and curated collections, and those with artistic restraint and high architectural interest. Always, however, luxurious and sustainable materials, handcrafted pieces, and old-school workmanship shine.

The spaces on these pages expertly navigate the dynamic push and pull between Toronto's heritage and modern sensibilities—a tension that has created a true design movement. This reimagining of existing housing stock that considers both traditional and contemporary creates exemplary homes that feel at ease in their settings, adding to the urban landscape for the next generation of Torontonians.

Studio 1Ninel's Bloorcourt project.

In my neighbourhood, for example, homes were originally designed for the working-class labourers building this city (practical but not luxurious). Then, for decades, they were occupied by multi-generational families, with kitchens on every floor. Next up were young urban couples looking to raise their families, living out their DIY reno dreams. And now there are upwardly mobile young owners who are tapping into the talent of the city's design professionals and renovating semis into modern dream homes with an elevated and worldly aesthetic. These houses have functioned successfully in every one of these eras, taking on new looks and configurations with each passing decade.

Toronto style favours individualism, quality over quantity, and high-concept interior architecture. It's also unabashedly practical (read: lots of gorgeous millwork and useful storage). Another thread that weaves its way through many of these incredible homes is beautiful staircases, whether they are heavy and sculptural or light and ethereal. This hard-working portion of our homes literally connects spaces, and was oft neglected in years past, especially in residences that were conceived as standard lower- or middle-class housing. The staircase is almost metaphorical to change, and provides a perfect opportunity to inject fresh energy and personality.

For this collection of Toronto studios working in residential design, I selected the ones that spoke to my heart on some level. They, too, differ from one another and even from project to project, which I think is key to "good design." Each of these studios listens to its clients and is sensitive to the landscape they are given to work within and, often, to the confines of an old house and City approvals. These thirty firms, which work across the city, also run the gamut from well established to neophyte in terms of number of projects under their belt, but each possesses a unique sensibility that is adding greatly to the look of the city's homes—one that applauds natural materials and local craftsmanship. I think one day Toronto's interior design aesthetic may be more easily seen from afar, but for now I cherish the diverse and layered feeling to our neighbourhoods and the people who live here.

In writing this, I was greatly motivated by two older books on my shelves—Terence Conran's iconic *The House Book*, cataloguing his interior design work, and *Bohemian Modern* by architect Barbara Bestor, capturing the many quirky and unique spaces in Silver Lake, Los Angeles. I hope that the homes in this book will inspire you to look at your own space differently, to dream of what's possible and embrace some of these ideas. Personally, what I love most is a home that's tailored to the idiosyncrasies of its inhabitants, something unique and warm and welcoming, something with colour and art, a bit of humour, and the beautiful imperfections of a life well lived.

Kim Lambert Design's Hoggs Hollow project.

Lisa Lev Design's Huron project.

# ACDO

THERE IS SOMETHING truly special about the homes designed by ACDO. You can see and feel it on many levels—the details and personal stories woven into their spaces speak to a high level of synergy between the designers and their clients. Long-time friends Abraham Chan and Sam Khouvongsavanh worked together for ten years at a high-end interior design studio in Toronto before branching out on their own. Both pursued degrees in architecture and then transitioned into interior design, finding a passion for its tactile nature and human-centric focus. Chan, who was born in Calgary but raised in Hong Kong, established ACDO nearly a decade ago, with Khouvongsavanh joining following a tenure in Singapore during the pandemic. Their combined international and local experience allows them to seamlessly integrate interior aesthetics with architectural rigour. Their projects defy convention with unique detailing and materials and thoughtful contemporary floor plans. From the interior architecture down to custom furniture design, art, and accessories, the studio is holistic in its approach. Now with ten members, ACDO has worked extensively in North America, Asia, and Europe—experience that brings with it a broad worldview. With a strong foothold in private residential projects, ACDO also crafts luxury hospitality, commercial, and retail properties, which have included Four Seasons Whistler, Avenue Road in Vancouver, and the Toronto office of X/Twitter. Lovers of art, culture, and music, Chan and Khouvongsavanh continually seek challenges to invigorate their creative spirit.

The home office of this Rosedale project is a creative exploration of natural materials and tones, highlighted by brass accents.

## Rosedale Colour

What started as a renovation of a few rooms evolved into a comprehensive transformation of a once-muted Rosedale home into a vibrant personal expression. Almost every space is reimagined with lush, saturated colour and a uniquely integrated material palette. The once-neutral interiors, clad in white oak panelling and limestone, have been infused with monolithic blocks of colour, reflecting the homeowner's desire for a space that honours its architecture while also reflecting her personality. Unique custom furniture and rugs fine-tune the project with exacting scale and a sense of calm. In the basement, the media room is a sea of summer-solstice blue with custom mural panels hand-painted by local studio Moss & Lam to capture the views at the owner's Georgian Bay cottage. Throughout, vibrant elements like pink onyx in the primary ensuite blend with the original architecture, crafting a space where elegance meets daring creativity.

Bold colour blocking continues throughout the home including dynamic panels custom-made by local studio Moss & Lam for the media room.

## Lake Views

Set on the shores of Lake Ontario, this residential project overhauled two separate penthouses into a luxurious 10,000-square-foot home with sweeping 180-degree views from the low-rise building. Inspired by luxury resorts the owner had visited in Asia, the design emphasizes a serene, spa-like atmosphere with intimate spaces leading to a dramatic double-height volume. The centrepiece is a wooden "cube" housing the kitchen and primary bedroom, symbolizing a glowing lantern around which the rest of the home revolves. In the primary bathroom, ACDO evokes a hammam-like setting replete with a living green wall. The project was executed with meticulous attention to detail, from structural changes to accessories. Ample natural light and recurring blue tones complement the lakeside setting, while beloved and carefully selected artwork and furniture, including Southeast Asian pieces and bespoke carpets, create a luxurious and warm environment.

The colour blue is a running feature in the home, which intentionally complements the lake beyond.

The large penthouse project adjoined two units into one.

Custom rugs are a signature of ACDO projects. Here, the swirls of blue are a natural segue from the natural stone.

The studio was aiming for a hammam-type experience in the principal suite, replete with a living green wall.

# ASHLEY BOTTEN DESIGN

**ASHLEY BOTTEN'S JOURNEY** into the world of design began long before she founded her eponymous studio in 2008. Growing up, she loved arranging and perfecting spaces—a passion that would later evolve into a career as a set stylist for film and television. After her first residential project, Botten honed her own design language. The studio takes a personal approach to design, rooted in the belief that a home should be an authentic reflection of its inhabitants. Material palettes, each one carefully curated, play a crucial role in the success of the studio's projects. Whether Botten is working with the warm glow of copper, the timeless elegance of oak, or the sculptural quality of bespoke furniture, her ability to harmonize textures and materials results in interiors that exude understated luxury while remaining welcoming and unpretentious. Using primarily natural materials and a contemporary eye, the studio creates spaces with a sense of warm luxury. Within these spaces is always a touch of whimsy that adds unexpected charm. It's a recipe that delivers homes that are both sophisticated and youthful. Complementing its residential interiors, the studio has its own line of timeless contemporary furniture crafted from natural materials. The pieces are showcased at their Toronto studio, which doubles as a semi-public showroom and a space for creative exploration.

An oval table from Collection Particulière pairs elegantly with classic Saarinen tulip chairs.

## Midtown Georgian

This renovation of a beloved Georgian home began with a deep respect for its historical roots, preserving classic features like stately mouldings and original doors while introducing a contemporary edge—new hardware, extended frames, and bold new lines. A harmonious blend of old and new emerges, where the front honours the home's heritage and the rear addition meets the needs of a modern family, including an ample side entrance. Natural finishes were chosen almost exclusively, with an earthy palette featuring oil-treated flooring, honed and leathered marble, anodized aluminum, and copper designed to age gracefully. The studio's design ethos prioritizes flow, with each space transitioning naturally into the next, unified by refined finishes and thoughtful meeting points between old and new. From a custom rug anchoring the foyer to bespoke furniture and sleek blackened-steel accents in the kitchen, every detail serves a purpose, making the home as functional as it is beautiful.

For the studio, the interplay between old and new is expressed most effectively in the door, window, and wall trims. Some are original, while others are modified to a more pared-down form for thoughtful and considered transitions.

The studio's design respects the history of the old home while modernizing each space. The clients were equally passionate about designing an interior that could outlast trends.

The home's principal suite is an unabashedly luxurious and serene escape.

PLENTY
LOVE & LEMONS
NATURALLY NOURISHED
OTTOLENGHI
MEXICO

# ASQUITH ARCHITECTURE

AWARD-WINNING ARCHITECT Heather Asquith's incredible eye and expertise make her a sought-after designer. She contributed at several established firms before branching out on her own in 2010 to specialize in modern residential design. The studio produces thoughtfully executed renovations that speak to each site and the people living there with a keen attention to detail. From framing views to celebrating the quirks of everyday life, the studio captures the essence of a warm, welcoming home within the envelope of clean, modern design. Asquith's time travelling and working in Finland greatly informs her aesthetic choices and approach to space planning. Much of her work is done on small-space Toronto homes, which has given her an ease with heritage elements, sustainability, and unique site constraints. By cultivating a meaningful connection to the places she works on, Asquith is able to achieve creative and practical solutions to almost anything. Her focus on material and colour adds a timelessness characterized by richness and depth.



With a client who was not shy about colour, Asquith Architecture and interior designer Julie Reinhart leaned into a bold and uplifting palette.

## Playter Estates

Working with interior designer Julie Reinhart, Asquith Architecture breathed new life into this hundred-year-old house with a vibrant palette. For a family of five who craved space and light, this wasn't just a makeover—it was a life-changing reinvention. Originally dark and closed off, the house benefited from floor-to-ceiling windows and an open, airy layout. The heart of the home is now the expansive kitchen, playfully finished in teal cabinetry, with pops of orange and yellow. Upstairs is reconfigured to add another bedroom and bathroom bubbling in cyan, yellow, and patterned floor tiles. A family playroom in the dug-out basement was crafted with fun secret hideouts for the kids. Throughout, the fresh, bright palette contrasts with warm European oak floors, while details like ombré stairs and custom lighting add personality.

Old meets new in this whole-home renovation that carves out an improved floor plan to optimize storage.

## Leslieville Reno

This bold renovation evolved as it went along, designed for a ceramic artist who fell in love with the raw beauty of the exposed brick once the house was stripped of its interior finishes. The decision to insulate the exterior and clad it in metal allowed the rustic brick to set the tone for a loft-like industrial aesthetic. Exposed wood floor joists add warmth and texture, creating a space that feels both raw and refined. The house is not just a living space but an artist's studio, with ceramics displayed throughout on custom shelving. The design honours the home's history with touches like exposed plaster walls, while the carefully coordinated copper piping and exposed ductwork add a sense of industrial artistry. A striking milled-steel staircase, illuminated by a skylight, serves as a sculptural centrepiece, and warm cabinetry in white oak brings balance to the exposed elements.

When the owner, a potter, saw her home stripped back during demolition and loved the aesthetic, the design shifted to embrace the building's raw structure.

## Scandi-Toronto Reno

While many people love and embrace Scandinavian style, this home artfully channels it into a serene, minimalist space. Finnish design influences abound, including a light wood and white palette and a less-is-more/quality-over-quantity approach. Throughout the architectural renovation and addition, the studio drew from the serene beauty of the Nordic landscape using a material palette of white oak and natural stone that's instinctively soothing. Key interventions include a one-storey rear addition and a complete rethink of the basement, ground, and second floors. The previously dark, enclosed house is now a bright and inviting retreat, ideal for family life and entertaining with its calming, timeless aesthetic that celebrates simplicity and the beauty of nature.

Heather Asquith's Scandinavian influences are on full display in this downtown renovation. Her keen eye for scale and material are both seen and felt in this minimal yet warm home.

# ATELIER SUN

FOUNDED BY INTERIOR DESIGNER Andrew Sun, Atelier Sun's designs blend Euro-Asian influences with the transformative power of spatial storytelling. The multidisciplinary studio blends old-world craftsmanship with a contemporary eye, fashioning spaces that touch the soul. Sun's philosophy is rooted in a desire to create beauty in unconventional ways through careful manipulation of natural and artificial light. His work is not just about design but about curating emotional responses and experiences. Each project begins with an order and symmetry that is then distorted through the artful use of light, challenging perceptions and evoking a deep, intuitive connection with the space. This approach allows Sun to craft environments that are at once surprising and harmonious—they embrace subtlety and sophistication, often drawing from the rich traditions of Asian design, while making those spaces accessible and relevant in North America. This sensitivity to diverse influences defines the studio's unique aesthetic, creating spaces that resonate with a global sensibility and remain deeply personal to each client. Collaboration is at the heart of Sun's approach, ensuring that each project is a true reflection of the client's story and lifestyle and meets their practical needs. In addition to its bespoke residential designs, Atelier Sun has put its stamp on hospitality, retail, and healthcare projects.



The studio optimizes built-ins and natural textures to maximize space in smaller homes.

## Harty House

What was once a cookie-cutter 1980s builder home is now a tranquil oasis with an understated natural palette. The studio faced the challenge of integrating seven awkwardly placed columns within the 850-square-foot floor area. Sun's approach minimized visual clutter, turning structural obstacles into elegant design features. To maximize space further, extensive built-ins inject a timeless elegance. The house embodies the studio's signature style—sleek, minimal, and warm. The foyer, wrapped in wood panels, seamlessly incorporates bench seating, a shoe rack, and a closet, while the floating staircase visually extends this millwork, creating a cozy, inviting atmosphere. A wood privacy wall adds a touch of sophistication, casting ever-changing shadows and subtly delineating spaces. The project reflects the studio's ability to transform ordinary spaces into serene, functional retreats, where every element is thoughtfully designed to elicit an emotional connection.

Working around many structural obstacles, the studio crafted a warm and inviting home clad in wood tones.

A unique partially open staircase is a highlight at Harty House.

## Gallery Home

This renovation is a testament to the harmonious interplay of form, light, and emotion. Crafted for a discerning art collector, the design transcends convention, offering a contemplative space where simplicity meets profound depth. Drawing inspiration from the paintings of Mark Rothko, the studio's plan activates a type of living canvas, shifting as the light moves throughout the day. Inside, the design speaks in whispers of elegance and restraint. White walls and white oak floors create a seamless canvas, while textured millwork and stone elements introduce layers of complexity. Natural light filters through the rooms, casting dynamic shadows that animate the space. When viewed from outside as dusk approaches, the white stucco façade transforms—the house softens and a warm, golden glow emanates from within.

Drama is on high at the Gallery house, designed with ample wall space for hanging art and thoughtful attention paid to light and shadow.

## The Courtyard House

Sun designed this East York home for a couple of creatives who wanted an urban oasis. Taking this craving quite literally, he gifted them a central bamboo courtyard—a feature that took some doing to pull off. Working with a landscape engineer, Sun achieved a dramatic and central focal point on the main level that defines the entire home. The design gives the feeling of an open-air courtyard without being open to the Canadian elements. Strategic skylights channel light deep into the narrow home. A cohesive palette in the studio's signature pale wood lays the foundation for the fresh and youthful home. Open risers and spindles, along with slatted partition walls and horizontal wall panelling, add geometry, structure, and movement.

A living bamboo garden was a structural feat in this home, one of its many Asian influences.

A large overhead skylight pulls light deep into the three-storey home.

# BARBORA VOKAC TAYLOR ARCHITECT

ARCHITECT BARBORA VOKAC TAYLOR is the creative force behind BVTA, where she blends her passion for architecture with a deep commitment to quality, well-being, and sustainability. With a rich background in both design and technical resolution, Vokac Taylor crafts spaces that don't just function—they resonate. BVTA's portfolio is as diverse as it is impactful, spanning residential, institutional, and commercial projects along with new builds, renovations, and interiors. What sets Vokac Taylor's work apart is her ability to balance tactile beauty and atmospheric richness with the practical demands of longevity and usefulness. Each project is a study in contrasts—where elegance meets common-sense sustainability, and every design decision is rooted in the human experience. Before launching her own practice, Vokac Taylor honed her craft alongside celebrated architects in Toronto, London, and Montreal, contributing to award-winning projects across many sectors. A dynamic presence in the design community, Vokac Taylor plays an active role in fostering dialogue and innovation through her involvement with the Toronto Society of Architects and the Design Industry Advisory Committee. She also shares her expertise as a part-time professor, guest critic, and program advisor, helping shape the next generation of architects.

BVTA expertly mixed materials and patterns for a lively palette in an open space.

## Summerhill Family Home

Located in one of the sweetest spots this city has to offer was a wonderful family home that just needed some updating. BVTA transformed the once dark and partitioned house into a vibrant, family-focused space with socializing in mind. The redesign included a full-gut renovation, a three-storey rear addition, and extensive landscaping that gracefully connects the house to its environment. The reimagined interior now flows from room to room, ideal for both intimate family moments and large gatherings. Custom millwork adds texture and interest while acting as a grounding backdrop for the family's contemporary art collection. Upstairs, serenity prevails, including in the principal suite, with a walk-through closet and a terrace overlooking the garden. One of the coolest parts of the home may be the sculptural steel screen on the rear elevation, offering privacy and a dynamic play of light.

On the rear façade, a unique weathered-steel lattice beautifully filters light inside.

A heated concrete floor steps up to create a designated conversation area.

The new street-facing dining room with a cozy banquette has views to both the kitchen and front foyer.

## Hibou House

This project saw a sprawling 1950s Etobicoke home transformed by a fresh, modern spin that's as stylish as it is practical. Departing from a traditional plan that results in smaller, disconnected rooms, the floor plan has a central observation point: the kitchen, with rooms radiating outward. This concept allows for an open, interconnected layout where the ground floor spaces are visually connected with the kitchen but still feel distinct. The result is a home that feels expansive and harmonious, with sightlines that create a sense of unity throughout and foster interaction while still providing individual areas of privacy and comfort. The family wanted a home that was perfect for entertaining friends of all ages, so BVTA crafted overlapping social-driven spaces, including a cozy breakfast nook and a basement rec room, designed for both family time and hosting guests. A sense of calm is cultivated with the understated material palette, which includes dark smoked oak floors and reeded walnut wainscotting that curves around the existing walls leading from one to the next. A single-storey addition at the rear is clad in blackened wood, a striking contrast to the bright interiors.

The home's thoughtful floor plan allows for connectivity with a kitchen designed for clients who love to cook together as a family.

Named after an owl, the Hibou house has vantage points from all angles. The large Etobicoke home was revitalized with the ideas of family and entertaining in mind.

# BATAY-CSORBA ARCHITECTS

IN 2008, following seven years in Los Angeles spent pursuing graduate degrees in architecture at UCLA, husband-and-wife duo Andrew and Jodi Batay-Csorba returned to Canada, setting up shop in Toronto. While in L.A., they worked with some of the most respected names in the field—Andrew at Morphosis and Jodi at Frank Gehry's firm, among others. Their illustrious portfolio has grown to include cultural institutions and multi-unit housing alongside their many residential projects, each characterized by a deep understanding of the unique qualities of the client, program, and site. They have become known for reigniting Toronto's historical use of masonry and evolving the craft into projects that take it somewhere new, creating a balance between blending in and standing out. Their work is distinguished by an exemplary execution of concept—a direct result of their commitment to exploring new ideas and pushing the boundaries of architectural design. The firm remains intentionally small, with a team of four to five, allowing the duo to maintain a hands-on approach to every project. With a design process that's best described as iterative, deeply personal, and layered with meaning, each home they design not only meets the client's needs but also resonates with the surrounding environments and communities.

A grand vaulted kitchen is grounded by warm, natural materials.

## Westminster House

Dramatic and unique, with a commanding presence and artfully laid-out interiors, this home is an ideal example of the new Toronto modern. The studio focused on a design that reflects the unique personalities and preferences of its owners. Inspired by the gable roofs of Edwardian homes in the neighbourhood, the design plays with scale and geometry, creating a loft-like second floor that feels magical and cozy. Set on a corner lot, the home maximizes daylight through a reoriented interior that opens onto a private, landscaped side yard. To satisfy one client's preference for dark dramatic spaces and the other's for bright, uplifting rooms, Batay-Csorba imagined a harmonious blend of contrasting styles elegantly expressed with moody, compressed areas leading into light-filled, open spaces.

The floor plan effortlessly connects all parts of the home.

## Humber Residence

Set on an irregularly shaped 65-by-20-foot corner lot, this family home was reimagined using the existing modest footprint. The studio maximizes the site with a vertical, four-storey plan centred on a light-filled stairwell, which creates an expansive feeling and unique, treehouse-like spaces in each bedroom. A beautifully carved-out deck offers sweeping views of the Humber River and a private retreat for the whole family. Baltic birch panelling and simple, durable materials like terrazzo and narrow-plank white oak flooring add warmth and livability to the space. The exterior is clad in historical buff yellow brick with subtle coursing patterns, giving the house a distinctive presence in the neighbourhood. This interplay between traditional materials and contemporary design principles translates to a home that is both timeless and uniquely tailored to the client's vision, a new gold standard for Toronto homes.

Taking advantage of the elevated corner lot, the design draws light deep into the home via various geometric cut-outs.

## High Park

A challenging lot and a need for a garage sparked the creative process for this High Park new build. Not wanting a garage to be the dominant force on the façade, the studio opted for a unique carport that's dramatically integrated into the entry sequence. The materiality of the project plays a starring role, with dark, richly textured brickwork that pays homage to Toronto's Victorian heritage while pushing the boundaries of modern design. A stunning barrel vault that runs the length of the house was inspired by the clients' love of Italian architecture and heritage. The vault isn't just a structural feature but a dynamic canvas, where light playfully interacts through strategic cut-outs and skylights, creating unique experiences as you move through the home. Inside, the contrast continues with serene white vaulted spaces that feel expansive yet intimate, thanks to clever spatial divisions.

A warm, enveloping interior is a result of the home's barrel-vault architecture.

PHOTO
WARHOL LIVE

# CHAPO DESIGN INC. | CHAPI CHAPO DESIGN

BORN AND RAISED IN PARIS, Boris Mathias studied architecture at the École Nationale Supérieure d'Architecture de Paris-Malaquais, where he earned his professional degree in architecture. This distinguished academic foundation, combined with his passion for design, has shaped his approach to crafting extraordinary spaces. Since its inception, Chapo Design Inc. has embraced the philosophy that interior design should transcend aesthetics and explore the profound impact of space on human experience. This guiding principle is evident in its meticulously curated portfolio, with projects that blend sophistication with functionality, catering to the discerning tastes of international clients.

A thoughtful use of lighting exemplifies the studio's philosophy where each component is not merely functional but a key design element, carefully calibrated to shape the atmosphere and evoke emotion. Similarly, the tactile quality of materials—from the finish of stones to the texture of fabrics—plays a crucial role in shaping the overall experience, ensuring each space resonates with warmth and refinement. Mathias is also a partner in Chapi Chapo Design, bringing decades of global experience to the studio. His work spans China, the Middle East, North and South America, Europe, Vietnam, India, Maldives, Japan, Bangladesh, and Hawai'i, informing a deeply collaborative process where attention to detail defines each project. The studio pushes the boundaries of luxury, delivering spaces that exemplify design's transformative power.

A chic formal dining room with ambient integrated lighting evokes a chef's private dining room in the studio's Rosedale project.

## Rosedale Residence

This classic centre-hall Georgian home was completely transformed into a dynamic, modern space layered in rich wood and textiles. Inspired by a deep understanding of the client's lifestyle, honed from a previous cottage project done together in Muskoka, the studio crafted a pitch-perfect redesign for this family that loves to make music. The heart of the transformation was opening the kitchen to the dining room to create an expansive flow that enhances both daily life and entertaining. Architectural touches like framed views, custom wood arches, and a floating wood ceiling add tremendous warmth and sophistication. The design preserves cherished elements, including an existing rolling ladder and bar panelling, while introducing new luxurious details, such as the moody caramel and grey colour palette and the custom stonework. Each room, from the music-filled living space to the serene principal bedroom and expansive bathroom, has been thoughtfully designed to be both functional and inviting, capturing the homeowner's rock'n'roll spirit with an upscale twist.

A sleek home bar with designated seating areas is perfect for the clients who love to listen to music with friends.

The primary suite is a welcome respite with luxurious finishes and integrated lighting.

## Cabbagetown Townhouse

A slender townhouse in Cabbagetown was overhauled with a playful and meticulous renovation for the owner of a high-end furniture store. An old greenhouse addition was ill suited to Canadian winters, so the transformation reconnected the space with the outdoors by blowing out the back façade and raising the roof for a lighter, airier feel. Inside, the kitchen was liberated from its cramped quarters, making room for serious cooking and custom cabinetry. The third floor saw the biggest change—flipping the bedroom to the back for a quieter, sunnier retreat, complete with a walnut tub and custom millwork in the bathroom. Uniquely, the living room doubles as an extension of the owner's showroom, a living lab where concealed storage, integrated lighting, and bold accents highlight an impressive art collection. Every detail, from the sliding panels to the stone and metal finishes, was carefully curated to blend function, elegance, and a European touch—all within a thoughtfully managed budget.

A narrow rowhouse is envisioned using dramatic finishes and a bold colour scheme, ideal for the homeowner, who owns a design showroom.

## Temple Residence

Nestled in a dynamic downtown neighbourhood, this multi-unit residential project on Temple Street epitomizes the studio's ability to craft luxury homes with ease. Created in collaboration with Curated Property (the client) and RAW Design (the architect), the thirteen-storey residence merges architecture and interior design with a holistic approach to public and private spaces. The community-focused design emphasizes fluidity; from the terracotta-hued arches framing the lobby to the flexible kitchen islands doubling as dining tables, every detail invites interaction. Informed by post-pandemic living, the design planned for several private enclaves, such as sophisticated phone booths for quiet work, alongside social spaces like the rooftop chef's kitchen, which extends into an open-air bar. The integration of a projection screen on the terrace transforms evenings with cinematic drama, emphasizing versatility through all seasons. A rich and textural palette is luxurious but warm and approachable, ideal for daily living, socializing, and working in the heart of the city.

At this multi-unit residential project, thoughtful details signal a truly unique home with an outdoor screen on the building's top-floor terrace.

The studio focused on designing highly functional and comfortable common spaces that evoke interaction between residents.

BON VOYAGE
THE KINFOLK HOME
LIVE BEAUTIFUL
at 100
THE KINFOLK HOME
ROCK THE SHACK

# COMMON GOOD STUDIO

BORN IN THE MIDST of a global shift, Common Good Studio emerged as an emblem of resilience and creativity in Toronto's design landscape. Conceived during the pandemic by a designer with roots in both anthropology and art history, the studio's ethos is uniquely grounded in an understanding of how people inhabit spaces and share experiences. Founder Natasha Popek-Konieczko, who honed her skills at influential firms and accumulated years of intensive learning, nurtured a profound ambition—to create spaces that resonate, where people don't just exist but thrive. From modest beginnings, Common Good Studio cultivated its practice with meticulous attention to detail, infusing each project with a blend of modernity and timelessness using organic materials and soothing patterns. Their projects are highly personal and speak to current styles while being grounded in the classics. Popek-Konieczko's fascination with human interactions, shaped by years of anthropological study, guides a practice that approaches each design as a narrative, seamlessly connecting people to the spaces they inhabit. Now nearing half a decade, the studio prides itself on a collaborative ethos, engaging local artisans and skilled trades to weave each client's unique story into the fabric of their environment. The studio's portfolio in both hospitality and residential represents a careful balance of innovation and heritage, tailored to reflect the essence of those who dwell within.



The studio's Annex renovation emphasized fluidity and brightness in this once dark home.

Merging classic and contemporary, the studio's plan for this renovation begins a new era for this century-old home.

## Annex Revival

In the heart of the Annex, this home breathes with the warmth of a bygone era elegantly revived. Once a shell of its history, this residence is now a testament to its architectural past updated for modern living. Striving to uphold the home's character, the original woodwork still graces the halls, glowing under gentle, restored light fixtures. The bathroom, reborn with a Japanese soaker tub, retains the splendour of its stained-glass accents. The multi-generational design embraces three families under one roof, a mosaic of shared and private spaces. On the second floor, a unique suite emerges, where walk-through closets lead to luxurious, connected rooms. The kitchen with its heritage blue hues is a natural draw. The design emphasizes utility and beauty with dual sinks, a workhorse range, and delicate glass hardware. Living areas mix classic Canadiana with playful touches, including reclaimed faucets and a low surfboard-style table. Adding to the fullness of the family-friendly design, open shelves overflow with photos, books, and games.

A Japanese soaker tub and spare, minimalist lighting pair beautifully with more traditional wall panels.

## Forest Hill North Family Home

Nestled in the esteemed enclave of Forest Hill North, this full-gut renovation and addition harmonize vintage elements and modern twists. Originally a 1960s build, its transformation epitomizes the seamless marriage of mid-century nostalgia and contemporary luxury. The home spans four split levels and celebrates a family's lively traditions, bustling energy, and deep-rooted values. A bold European-inspired powder room and the strategically enhanced kitchen bring both function and beauty to the design. Fluted columns and Parisian-inspired mouldings evoke the elegance of old-world architecture paired with a sleek, modern take on the millwork. Brass fixtures, subtly aged to develop a patina over time, speak to this enduring style, while deeper hues balance the overall airiness of the house. Attention to detail extends into the dining room where full-height glass-fronted cabinets frame Judaica treasures and a handwashing sink, paying homage to the family's Shabbat rituals. The living room, grounded with symmetry and charm, offers the ideal oasis for quiet evenings. The studio gave new life to this once-bland space while uniquely weaving in family traditions.

The redesign of this 1960 home effortlessly merges mid-century lines with the family's contemporary collections.

## High Park Style

This Georgian-era residence had benefited from an open-concept transformation by a previous owner, marked by thoughtful architectural updates, including a steel column supporting the heart of the home. Yet the kitchen lingered in the past with dated aesthetics and disjointed ceiling heights. Meeting the family—a dynamic couple with two children—sparked the studio's vision for a refreshed space that balances sophistication with practicality. Despite the owner's initial preference for an all-white kitchen, the design evolved into a study of subtle contrasts using organic tones and materials. A striking kitchen island of green-stained white oak introduces natural texture, juxtaposed with smooth quartz countertops and unique tile accents. The space now effectively caters to a busy, vibrant life where custom storage conceals everyday essentials and there are dedicated coffee and smoothie zones. In the dining room, sleek millwork provides practical solutions for stashing children's items while reserving areas for a curated display. The studio captured the home's original charm while beautifully contemporizing it for family life.

A soft organic palette offers a fresh take on the usual classic white kitchen. The studio merged modern and classic pieces for a comfortable family setting.

## Laid-Back Leslieville

In the city's east end stands a semi-detached home reborn in an elegant, contemporary style. The clients, who are passionate about design, yearned for cohesion in their open-concept space—a place that would embrace the vibrant chaos of family life while exuding a refined charm when hosting friends. The original brick wall, rich with character, became a feature element, framing the reoriented living room. Discreet toy storage is tucked under the stairs. In the dining room, flowerpot pendants offer bursts of colour suspended like playful art and pair with the home's curated collections. The kitchen, which was once constrained by an awkward peninsula, was liberated into an expansive space with floor-to-ceiling cabinetry and built-in appliances. A new island clad with white-oak shiplap anchors the kitchen as a place to gather, while the sandy, beach-inspired palette breathes tranquility into each room. Millwork throughout balances open display with concealed storage, ensuring the home's elegance remains uncluttered in the face of busy family life.

DELI
THANKS FOR
THE EGGS
LADIES
STOP HAVING A
BORING TUNA.
STOP HAVING A
BORING LIFE.
FETTUCCINE.
LINGUINE.
MARTINI.
BIKINI.

# DART STUDIO

FOUNDED BY DESIGNER Olivia Botrie, Dart Studio brings both wonderful refinement and playfulness to its residential projects, which balance the preservation of original architectural details with the storage needs of contemporary life. The studio's work is characterized by thoughtful space planning and a sophisticated approach to colour and texture, often layering heritage elements with bold and modern colour and pattern. With expertise in reimagining traditional Toronto homes, Dart deftly reconfigures floor plans to maximize functionality without compromising architectural integrity. Botrie and her team, which includes sister Jenna Botrie, are known for their curated material palettes that emphasize warmth and tactility, from patinated brass to richly textured wallcoverings. Olivia's background in television production and prop styling informs her keen eye for detail and ability to layer spaces with meaning. Dart excels at creating environments that feel carefully considered and effortlessly lived in, incorporating clients' art collections and personal elements with ease. Their work consistently shows a deep understanding of how homes need to function for busy families while maintaining an elevated and artistic sensibility.



A curated gallery wall and custom banquette make for a cozy and considered breakfast nook.

## Roncesvalles V

A comprehensive renovation transformed this original but neglected Toronto home into a sophisticated backdrop for the owner's notable Canadian art collection. The project involved significant spatial reconfiguration, including relocating the staircase to create better flow and maximize storage opportunities. Using a material palette that centres on warm neutrals, the design perfectly reflects the client's long-standing personal aesthetic preferences. In the kitchen, the banquette seating area with a curated gallery wall is a natural draw on the main floor. Practical considerations like porcelain-tile flooring in high-traffic areas accommodate the reality of living with large, active dogs but don't take away from the aesthetics. Custom millwork throughout provides abundant storage while cultivating a seamless and coherent envelope. The design team paid particular attention to preserving original architectural elements where possible, such as incorporating period-appropriate fireplaces in new locations. The result is a home that feels both historically grounded and thoroughly contemporary.

Surface detailing like the textured wall in the bathroom and painted wall in the children's room instantly add dimension and style.

## Roncesvalles VII

Heritage and modernity merge in this house, which was reinvented with fresh, imaginative expression. The full-gut renovation transformed an old rooming house into an intimate family home without adding square footage, instead relying on meticulous reorganization of the existing layout to foster both flow and intimacy. Embracing cozy spatial delineation, the design resists open-concept trends, preferring to craft rooms rich in atmosphere and individuality. Lovers of colour and texture, Botrie and her team filled each space with thoughtfully chosen wallpapers, allowing pattern to wrap walls and ceilings, embracing the architectural quirks of the house. Custom built-ins, such as a window bench under a sloping ceiling, offer both function and charm, while the kitchen's rich oak and subtle tones add a grounding, natural warmth to the heart of the home. The traditional-meets-modern design creates a deeply personal, layered living space that feels rooted, cozy, and timeless.

The studio used every opportunity to inject colour into this full-gut renovation, including coloured cabinetry and three types of wallpaper on the main floor.

## Bloor West II

This project demonstrates the studio's ability to elevate a previously renovated space through careful architectural intervention and refined material selections. The design expanded the original rear addition of the house to full width, creating a generous and cohesive living space. A key move involved rotating the staircase to create a more logical circulation pattern and enable a full wall of kitchen millwork and a central entryway from the back of the home. The material palette showcases the studio's sophisticated approach to texture and warmth, featuring a striking custom brass hood vent with a specialized patina, marble-look porcelain countertops, and integrated mudroom storage that appears as an extension of the kitchen millwork. Drama is added in small but mighty doses, like in the powder room, which is clad in Kelly Ventura's artistic wallcoverings. The primary bedroom, finished in rich brown tones, creates a cocooning effect while maintaining the home's overall sense of warmth and sophistication.

Once derelict, this family home was reinvigorated with tactile finishes and a deep, welcoming palette.

Custom storage in the entryway and bathrooms keeps the space in order.

## Broadview Beauty

Just off Broadview on the city's east end, this house was originally a classic Toronto home with closed, compartmentalized rooms. The studio's vision reimagined its interior flow to accommodate modern family life and frequent entertaining. A signature style of the studio, the enduring design beautifully marries timeless charm with a touch of whimsy, layering in textiles, organic materials, and soothing colours. With the future in mind for a family with three young children, the layout prioritizes flexible spaces that will effortlessly evolve with their needs. Strategic structural changes were key, such as reorienting the stairs to create a more graceful entryway. An additional mudroom area keeps the home organized, while custom cabinetry and abundant storage ensure clutter-free, welcoming spaces. Open kitchen and dining spaces invite leisurely connections, ideal for the ebb and flow of both entertaining and daily life.

Fluted millwork in the kitchen, plush seating, patterned textiles, and the seamless integration of custom cabinetry throughout create a sense of organic calm in this east-end home.

# EM DESIGN STUDIO

EMD STANDS AS A beacon of refined luxury and sophistication. Founded more than twenty years ago by Elizabeth Metcalfe, the studio has grown into a leading design practice in Toronto, well known for its timeless interiors that are created exclusively for every client's personal taste and style. Now, under the leadership of Nicole Webster and Natalia Stawecki, who have both been part of the studio for more than a decade, it continues to be one of Toronto's most coveted design firms. The studio embraces a modern and meaningful concept of luxury—one rooted in refinement, curation, and the unexpected. Their approach redefines luxury as an intimate connection to the spaces we inhabit, where beauty, simplicity, and exemplary craftsmanship are paramount. Their work is distinguished by its meticulous attention to detail, where every element is carefully considered. Each project is a testament to the studio's dedication to sourcing and collaborating with artisans who share their commitment to creating homes that will stand the test of time. Colour plays a pivotal role in the studio's design language, with palettes that are understated yet complex, to evoke a sense of harmony and balance. As EM Design Studio believes that people experience an emotional connection to the objects and spaces that surround them, their goal is to create beautiful homes that feel innately personal and welcoming.

A gentle organic palette pairs perfectly with soft, rounded custom furniture that inspires long, comfortable get-togethers.

## Private Residence

Surrounded by mature trees, this beautiful home designed by architect Richard Wengle speaks to classical design in a modern context. Creating a relationship between the exterior architecture and interior was fundamental to the studio's vision. High ceilings with dramatic traditional mouldings create a feeling of grandeur, while the detailing, furnishings, and millwork impart a decidedly contemporary feel. A palette of rich terracotta, soft lavender, and muted greens is contrasted by textural neutrals and black accents. The result is a sophisticated, classically inspired contemporary home for a young family. Anchored in the centre of the home is a magnificent spiral staircase topped with an eight-inch oculus, allowing light to flood in. The family room's pared-back fireplace and furnishings balance the architectural detailing, which continues into the kitchen and breakfast area. At the front of the house, Pierre Paulin's classic Ribbon Chair pairs beautifully with vintage Murano-glass sconces and a family-heirloom console.

Light filters through Pierre Frey draperies silhouetting a collection of deep green ceramic pieces that echo the soft-emerald quartzite.

## Rosedale

Rosedale is one of Toronto's oldest neighbourhoods, known for its winding trails, wild roses, and some of the city's loveliest homes. A full renovation exposed the beauty of the homeowner's ravine lot and opened opportunities to transform the house into a modern, sophisticated family-friendly space with a very personal and distinctive point of view. Beautiful natural finishes play a tremendous role in this home, with clay-based paints, oiled floorboards, plaster details, and richly veined marble. Simple geometric shapes were paired with soft, curvaceous furnishings, statement light fixtures, iconic vintage pieces, and one-of-a-kind artisan-crafted objects. Creating moments of beauty is key to the studio's design philosophy. The principal bathroom, with blond oak flooring and layered with a soft alpaca rug, was the perfect opportunity for a statement tub and cashmere drapery. In the dining room, a hand-finished clay wall finish in a deep inky blue contrasts with a ceiling wrapped in a soft blush wallcovering. The living room is refined yet welcoming for the family to enjoy, and the adjacent sunroom's expansive windows filter sunlight through hand-woven blinds, creating an immediate connection to the ravine below.

The fireplace feature in this unique design is shared by the rooms on both sides of the wall.

In the bathroom a daring green tub is dramatically highlighted by striated marble walls.

A classic sunroom with a dropped wood ceiling increases the cozy indoor-outdoor feeling of this classic home.

# GILLIAN GILLIES INTERIORS

GILLIAN GILLIES'S JOURNEY into the world of interior design began in her hometown of Edinburgh, Scotland, where she honed her skills before relocating to Canada in 2002. Her design philosophy is rooted in the belief that a home must be more than just a beautiful space; it must be a sanctuary that cradles its inhabitants. She designs with a keen awareness of how her clients live, ensuring that every room is both functional and inviting, not merely a showpiece. Her work is soulful, layered, and a touch eclectic. Pets, children, and the everyday bustle of life are all considered, leading to spaces that are not just seen but fully lived in. Colour, for Gillies, is a language of its own. She eschews the monotony of "greige"—an anti-colour that was all the rage when she first moved to Toronto. Her studio's projects are rife with pattern and rich, saturated hues that soothe and nurture—a welcome departure from the stark, impersonal spaces that often dominate modern interiors. Lovers of European and British design (and design magazines) will see why her work is sought after here in Canada. While residential design remains her primary focus, with a particular expertise in substantial renovation and new construction, Gillies is expanding into boutique hospitality and commercial spaces.



A warm mix of textural details defines this Lawrence Park home.

## Lawrence Park

Unapologetically bold, this interior renovation was born from the client's love of colour and trust in the artistic process. With surprises at every turn, the home unfolds, revealing both moments of quiet and artistic flair. Though compact, the entryway delivers a striking first impression with its unexpected ceiling wallpaper, setting a daring tone. The kitchen, subtly neutral, leads to a family room vibrant in a bold green wallpaper. Gillies likes to start each design with a textile and then work back to the practicalities. Each room layers comfort with beauty. In the principal suite, botanical wallpaper and a unique pendant fixture with arms reminiscent of branches are nods to the garden outside.

From the ceilings to the upholstery to the walls and floors, Gillies applies pattern and colour to animate every space.

## Kingsway

This Kingsway condominium underwent a transformative renovation, tailored to provide enduring comfort for the client. With a design centred on a harmonious open-concept plan suitable for social gatherings, the condo feels like a larger house. Walls between the kitchen and dining area were removed, making way for an elegant archway and ample storage. A once-cramped laundry room was expanded by taking over the old powder room, making it easier and more enjoyable for the owner to use. Lighting played a pivotal role, with carefully selected fixtures adding warmth and character throughout. To preserve sightlines, a hidden downdraft fan was incorporated into the kitchen. Gillies designed unique custom furnishings, often rounded, to further ease traffic flow. The art-filled living room is a perfect spot to curl up and relax, with a TV discreetly tucked away at one end.

A condominium that feels like a house thanks to beautiful and functional transition zones and interior detailing.

This Kingsway condominium was completely overhauled to highlight the owner's art collection.

## Summerhill

Long-time clients wished to renovate their city residence into a fresh, modern, yet familiar space. The principal bathroom became a masterpiece, with custom cherry-blossom wallpaper by British studio de Gournay. The design was originally hand-sketched by the studio, with branches elegantly radiating from a central ceiling light. Colours from the wallpaper flow seamlessly into the room, complementing the Italian lace curtains and luxurious Japanese soaking tub, complete with a heated backrest and hydrotherapy jets. In the shower, multiple jets and colour therapy offer an immersive experience. A stunning wall sconce, resembling a delicate earring, adds a touch of glamour, while the studio's unique "bracelet chair" is designed to wrap around the user like a beautiful cuff.

Beautiful custom wallpaper and Italian lace curtains in the principal suite are unabashedly feminine.

# GREAT LAKE STUDIO

FOUNDED BY ARCHITECT Rick Galezowski, this architecture and interior design practice is deeply rooted in fostering connections—between family members and with the natural world. The studio uniquely captures the essence of place, while elevating the experience of those who inhabit them. Galezowski's profound affinity for the natural world is evident in every project—from the warmth of the natural materials used, to their integration with the streetscape. His designs reflect a life spent in communion with nature, exploring remote landscapes on bicycle and paddling through the Great Lakes with his family. This bond with the outdoors informs his vision, making spaces that are not only architecturally significant but also instinctively comfortable. The studio pays meticulous attention to the specifics of a building's environment, with a keen eye for framing views and responding to the contours of the terrain. An artful use of daylight is a hallmark of the studio's work, transforming spaces with the movement of light and shadow. Every phase of a project is approached with care and collaboration, ensuring that the result is a building of exceptional quality, uniquely personal to its occupants, and a joy to live in. Often, the studio uses spaces that would otherwise be overlooked to great effect, such as an office overlooking the floor below, gaining valuable square footage and increasing a sense of connection.

Typical of Toronto semis, this home was very narrow. A unique divider wall and fireplace create the ultimate welcoming entryway.

## Bickford Park Residence

This project represents a bold reinvention of a classic downtown Toronto home, one that pushes the boundaries of its original, confined semi-detached footprint. By embracing the verticality of the space, the renovation transforms a family home for the next generation. The studio's focus was creating a sculptural, interconnected environment that belies the home's square footage. With the integration of a vertical light well that carves open the core of the home, natural light cascades throughout. The home reveals itself gradually through clever design elements like a minimal steel and glass staircase and hidden nooks. A uniquely positioned fireplace built into the foyer's oak cabinetry is a welcoming gesture that is visible from the entryway, living room, and kitchen. The studio mixed in many unexpected moments of delight, such as a cleverly concealed powder room, a small study upstairs, and a floating platform designed to hold plants at the foot of the staircase.

The studio is known for its creative use of every square foot. Here, an office nook is created in the upstairs landing.

Upstairs, a warm wood palette, greenery, and ample natural light bring nature indoors.

## Wedgewood Park Residence

A multi-generational home in Etobicoke successfully meets all the needs of a family of seven while maintaining a sense of privacy and tranquility. The new home, which replaced a small bungalow, blends harmoniously into its surroundings with its charred and oiled cedar cladding. The interior architecture was driven by the family's wish list, which required spaces for school-age children and a live-in suite for the grandparents. On the ground floor, the studio emphasizes flow and movement with open living, dining, and kitchen areas that are connected yet distinct. Upstairs, in contrast, is vertically oriented with compact rooms that feel spacious thanks to vaulted ceilings and skylights. A restrained material palette of grey elm cabinetry, white oak floors, and grey quartz counters creates a calm backdrop for family life. Every element of the home was designed by the studio for a happy and efficient living experience for all.

Home for a multi-generational family involved creating central meeting points and several spaces for privacy and retreat.

## Bellwoods Lodge

Nestled on a compact lot near the Ossington strip, this three-storey residence is a meticulously crafted urban sanctuary designed to foster close-knit family life and celebrate the outdoors. Rick Galezowski and his wife, architect Maggie Bennedsen, devised the plan—a split-level design revolving around a three-storey light well that bathes the interiors in natural sun and moonlight, creating an ever-present connection to the sky. The living spaces unfold across three distinct axes: the ground-level Garden Axis, the third-level Sky Axis, and the vertical Sun Axis, each connecting the house to nature for this family of outdoor enthusiasts. At the rear, privacy intensifies with subtle level changes and low partitions. A top-floor living room, perched in the treetops, offers a cozy, cabin-like atmosphere with a wood stove and a cedar ceiling, while the rooftop terrace offers panoramic views of the city skyline.

Making the most of the three-storey narrow house, the studio used built-ins and unique space planning to create a retreat in the heart of the city.

# IZEN ARCHITECTURE

THIS ALL-WOMEN STUDIO focuses on holistic designs in which every part of the home is considered as interconnected. From the first impression at the street to the foyer and beyond, Izen's work is cognizant of how space influences one's experience in it. The studio strives to craft houses that feel like personal sanctuaries, creating feelings of luxury, comfort, and safety. Many details go into achieving this, including having highly customized storage solutions to keep a home neat or having natural materials that are calming to the eye and spirit. Though all the studio's projects are geared to the clients' needs, there are unmistakable signature Izen moves—jaw-dropping staircases, integrated lighting, slatted panelling, and seamless connections between indoor and outdoor spaces. An affinity for nature is paramount to their success, with floor plans that frame key views or even a singular tree. By consciously selecting natural materials, such as walnut and marble, and working with indirect natural lighting to enhance architectural features, the studio creates comfortable, inviting living spaces, all with a touch of drama. While rooted in residential design, Izen Architecture also takes on select commercial projects, often for clients who have experienced its residential work. From dental offices to restaurants, the studio creates commercial environments that resonate with the same warmth and attention to detail that define its large body of residential work.

Izen used a mix of materials to achieve the unique and funky vibe in this Forest Hill renovation.

## House 21

Instead of gutting this funky mid-century house in Upper Forest Hill Village, the studio thoughtfully reimagined it while honouring its original architecture. This restorative approach preserved and repurposed key elements of the original design, including the original terrazzo floor in the foyer, and an intricate screen repositioned as a front-hall mirror wired with sconces—a dramatic artistic gesture that maintains the vintage appeal of the piece while adding functionality. In the kitchen, you'd never guess that the original hardware was preserved and repurposed, given how seamlessly it integrates into the new design. Rich walnut millwork and exposed brick continue the mid-century story, adding in new storage and seamless doors. To contemporize the home, much of the floor plan was reconfigured, but the result is not fully open concept or untrue to the home's era.

A restorative approach to this renovation resulted in a unique mid-century-inspired modern aesthetic.

An original screen from the mid-century home was repurposed in the front hall.

Each bathroom has its own unique aesthetic, where the studio has used geometric forms to great effect.

## House 49

Drama and craftsmanship collide in this Cedarvale renovation, which saw a grand family home meticulously reinvented. Upon entry, you are met with bold hand-carved wooden wall panelling, seamless integrated doors, and a floating concrete bench. The staircase is a showstopper, with a recessed wood handrail and burnished brass. The visually striking geometry of the stairs and the panelling is unexpected yet will surely stand the test of time. Adding to the mix of materials is sleek grey glass and a continuous lighting feature that leads you from one level to the next. In the kitchen, a massive Pietra grey island is offset by a stunning terrazzo backsplash. A large hidden pantry provides ample storage. Out back, a cabana with a built-in barbecue and integrated speakers sets the stage for easy indoor-outdoor living.

This large family home was reimagined using bold natural materials and a healthy dose of drama.

# KIM LAMBERT DESIGN

**KIM LAMBERT DESIGN** is a distinguished full-service interior design firm established in 2007 and known for crafting highly personalized spaces. With a focus on residential projects and, more recently, furniture design, the studio has a guiding philosophy to create environments that resonate emotionally with their inhabitants. Drawing on more than twenty years of experience, much of it rooted in the realm of global luxury and boutique hospitality design, Kim Lambert's work is defined by a contemporary sensibility that balances sophistication with expert restraint. Her designs come together with a beautiful choreography of materials, texture, and light, resulting in homes that are both timeless and soulful. Ornamentation is used with great intentionality, allowing each design element to quietly harmonize without disrupting the overall composition. At the heart of Lambert's creative process is a commitment to understanding her clients on a deeper level; by encouraging them to step just outside of their comfort zones, she is able to create spaces that are visually striking but also meaningful. Collaborating with an established network of artisans, architects, and specialized craftspeople, the studio brings to life bespoke creations for every project. Lambert transcends formulaic approaches, thriving on ideation, artistic exploration, and a constant sense of curiosity. The studio's projects not only fulfill their functional purpose but also tell a unique and captivating story.

Kim Lambert at her Republic of Rathnelly project.

## The Republic of Rathnelly

Located in the heart of one of the city's more unique neighbourhoods, the Republic of Rathnelly, this home is the epitome of quiet sophistication. The studio's subtle yet edgy design reflects the owners' love of calm interiors and their travels through Asia. The design brief called for a serene space, drawing inspiration from Japan, including principles of wabi-sabi—the beauty in imperfection and the passage of time. Flat-cut oak veneer, a focal material in the project, is used for the millwork throughout the home. Upon entering, one is greeted by a foyer lined in smoky wood slats, a striking unfolded origami staircase, and open sightlines that gently transition into more intimate spaces. The contemporary marble-clad fireplace adds warmth and coziness to the living areas, where thoughtful touches like delicate yet resilient Canadian-made string chairs around the dining table bring a sense of balance. This home, designed for a young family, moves between open expanses and cozy nooks, embracing minimalism without sacrificing warmth.

Warm and moody, this home renovation unfolds with a continuous palette of smoky greys.

## Annex

In Toronto's Annex neighbourhood, this century-old home underwent a transformative redesign, blending heritage with modern luxury. The client sought to honour the home's historical charm while giving it a fresh new contemporary vernacular. The result is a timeless balance where past and present coexist harmoniously. Embracing a modern Belgian aesthetic, the design wraps the home in monochromatic oak, unifying the floors and millwork for a seamless, understated elegance. Stunning tempest-blue stone slabs, inspired by the garden, ground the kitchen, while the restored original fireplace in the library anchors the home's heritage narrative. Every detail has been meticulously considered, from the custom millwork and decorative hardware to the lighting language, all of which create an intriguing ambience. Moving through the house, you experience a shift from preservation in the front to sleek modernity in the back, where contemporary touches like a custom copper range hood and slat walls add tactile character.

The long-time owner wanted to revive this century-old home with a modern focus.

## Hoggs Hollow

Set on a river in prestigious Hoggs Hollow, this family home blends minimalism with an otherworldly charm. The design creates a seamless flow between the enchanting and the rustic, realized through rich textures, bold forms, and unexpected contrasts. The interior language is one of quiet luxury, with layers of luxe velvet, silk, Venetian plaster, and hot-rolled steel creating striking juxtapositions. The kitchen is anchored by opulent Calacatta marble, offset by bold blackened oak cabinetry. Large windows frame serene views of the surrounding landscape, while the open floor plan fosters a sense of lightness despite the dramatic palette. Black-framed doors separate the hallways from the kitchen, offering the option to close off spaces for more intimate gatherings. In the living spaces, bespoke furniture and dramatic light fixturesby designers such as Apparatus Studio, Gabriel Scott, Michael Anastassiades, and Lee Broom give the design an edgy sophistication, making this Tudor-style home an exquisite blend of refinement and lived-in beauty.

Channelling a boutique hotel, this luxurious home hits all the key elements of a forever home.

# KOHN SHNIER ARCHITECTS



ESCHEWING TRENDS AND CONFORMITY, Kohn Shnier has been a stalwart in Toronto since 1990, when it was founded by Martin Kohn and John Shnier. Before the pair combined their talents, Kohn worked at OMA in Rotterdam and Shnier was awarded Canada's first-ever Prix de Rome in Architecture following his time at KPMB. They have more than made good on their initial plan to deliver design excellence through creative solutions. The studio is now a team of ten and boasts a vast portfolio that has been widely recognized, including nominations for several prestigious international awards and a spot in the Museum of Modern Art in New York. Closer to home, KSa has put its stamp on iconic Toronto buildings, including major renovations at the University of Toronto's University College, the iridescent Umbra Concept Store on John Street, and dozens of single-family and multi-unit residential projects that employ its signature use of materials and sleight of hand. Through reflective and refractive materials, many of the studio's projects possess an ethereal quality where light is used as a paintbrush, often concealing practicalities or balancing spaces visually. Based on the principles and approaches established by Martin Kohn and John Shnier, the studio is currently led forward by Maggie Bennedsen and Amin Ebrahim.

A custom table and chairs designed by founding partner John Shnier has seating for eight, and the ample dining area provides views of the client's art collection.

## Rosemary House

This Forest Hill home stays with you long after you visit—its layout, refined finishes, and feelings of warmth and comfort are palpable from the moment you step inside. With built-in furniture and a custom table designed by founding partner John Shnier, the newly built home focuses on human interaction. Upstairs, a central volume houses a bathroom and storage while creating a continuous path of circulation. Despite the option to build a much larger home, the decision was made to create a space that feels both expansive and cozy, making it ideal for a family of six. With slight changes in elevation, material shifts, and impactful details like a pleated ceiling, a tapered oak column, and integrated linear lighting for an extensive art collection, every space is demarcated with texture and character. The sunken living room has a natural draw leading seamlessly to the backyard. On the exterior, KSa's signature use of mirror balances the façade and reflects the greenery beyond.

This new build is perfectly aligned on its plot and optimizes its curves and angles.

## Tile House

Nobody does tile like this. This four-storey Midtown home for a couple of active empty nesters is a master class in pushing architectural boundaries while respecting tradition. Nestled among its Victorian neighbours, the home subtly redefines the rules with a façade of red clay that sets it apart yet respectfully fits into the streetscape. The home boasts a vertical layout on a sloped site that prioritizes stunning views as well as privacy. Inside, spaces are connected in surprising ways, with strategically placed openings that create a dialogue between levels. The materials, the movement of light through space, and the seamless unfolding of rooms are testaments to the thoughtful, considered approach that the studio brings to its architecture and interior design projects. Luxurious finishes include a neatly edited Bulthaup kitchen and extensive millwork along the west wall on each floor. The design is a harmonious blend of challenge and opportunity, where every constraint was turned into a creative triumph.

The Tile House completely reimagines the typology of the neighbourhood.

## Croft House

Often hailed as the original Toronto laneway house, the Croft house exemplifies innovative design on a constrained urban site. Despite its reputation, it was never truly a laneway house; the Little Italy property always had a dwelling, with remnants of the original foundation and walls integrated into the current build. The studio chose to create an "upside-down" layout, with the bedrooms and office on the ground floor and an expansive open-plan living area upstairs. The space, flooded with natural light and views from every direction, gives the illusion and feeling of a much larger home. Uniquely, a walled Japanese-inspired garden just six feet wide creates an enchanting and private view from the bathtub. A bathroom accessed off the mid-stair landing and tucked under the kitchen counter is but one of the many clever design solutions, including mirrors and concealed storage, that maximize every square inch of the small home.

The studio uses every square foot of smaller homes to great advantage.

## Dovercourt House

In Bloorcourt Village, this small city home exemplifies how thoughtful design can transform an urban space into a serene, light-filled sanctuary. Originally a piano store, the house, which is pressed up against the sidewalk, initially had a fishbowl feel about it, but lush cedars outside now form a natural screen, filtering light and noise while providing privacy. A unique dynamic is created inside by a side-yard entrance, something the studio does often, which allows the front area to remain at full width and bathed in natural sunlight. A central staircase, illuminated by a skylight, divides the house into distinct, functional halves. With airy rooms on either side, a sense of expanse is created in this narrow home. The studio was able to capitalize on the structural integrity of the old piano store, which was built to withstand the weight of several pianos, and include heated polished concrete floors throughout.

# LISA LEV DESIGN

ORIGINALLY FROM WINNIPEG, Lisa Lev grew up surrounded by the world of design and knew early on that interior design was her calling. For decades, from Winnipeg to Montreal and now Toronto, she has been crafting character-filled homes that are equal parts elegance and ease of living. Lev has perfected the art of the highly functional family home with a holistic approach that balances each client's current and future needs. Her liberal use of colour and unexpected pairings are a joy to experience. Uplifting and creative, Lev's designs are truly unique in their execution. This, complemented by her use of high-quality materials and craftsmanship, gives her spaces a resolved quality that intrinsically feels balanced and good for the soul. Specializing in residential renovations, Lev and her team effortlessly modernize historical spaces without taking away from a home's provenance. The studio is equally well versed in high-end contemporary spaces, always layering in texture and colour to achieve their signature warm, welcoming environments.

Lisa Lev embraces bold palettes and natural textures in her Richview project.

## Richview

Textures, colours, and avant-garde and boho pieces come together in a symphony of delight in this Forest Hill Village home. The focus of the project was to create a warm family home with a Mediterranean flavour. Several seating areas cultivate distinct conversation zones, ideal for both family life and entertaining, including a cozy banquette. Lev and her team were able to reimagine this space in a contemporary and comfortable style—with distinct nods to the past. The kitchen island and cabinetry are beautifully detailed and highly functional with both open and closed storage. The island's eating area can easily accommodate several diners, with an unexpected wide columnar base adding to the playful geometry of the room. Colourful handcrafted light fixtures and a mix of upholstery patterns are used to reinforce the home's layered and warm aesthetic.

Layers of colour and patterns abound to create a uniquely personal home.

## Huron

Old meets new perfectly in this large-scale renovation in the Annex. One owner loves modern and clean lines, while another cherishes antiques and sentimental pieces. Lev's studio was able to marry the two aesthetics in a way that's equal parts charming and fashion forward. The living room itself is a master class in furnishing, with of-the-moment and classic modern pieces sitting happily together in the traditional shell. Original flooring was refurbished and extended into the kitchen with eye-pleasing texture and richness. Using her trademark colour and unexpected pieces, Lev cultivated a home that's rich in the clients' history and taste while fully stepping into the future.

One owner loves modern, the other traditional, so the studio crafted this perfectly balanced interior to satisfy both.

## Bracondale

When Lisa Lev first visited this gracious old Hillcrest home, it did not have a speck of colour, pattern, or fun. But Lev knew the clients very well, including their love of colour, and was easily able to conjure a different vision for the space—one that would create a lively, welcoming home dripping in personality. In order to carve out much-needed closet space in the entryway without knocking down walls, she had to get creative, borrowing space from the adjacent living room to fit in uniquely rounded cabinets clad in fluted white oak. Elsewhere, texture and colour were layered, including in the green sunroom off the living room, which is a favourite spot for morning coffee and end-of-day lounging. Lev's design accents the home's more traditional rooms, making them more casual with fun wallpaper prints and a bold, happy-making palette.

A bland home is reinvigorated with bold patterns and sculptural built-ins.

## Clarendon

In this South Hill project, the owner's extensive travels are celebrated in a layered and bold globally inspired design. Every corner whispers of journeys taken, memories made, and stories shared. Lev deftly blends modern elements with cherished antiques. A sleek glass staircase contrasts beautifully with the warmth of wide-plank oak floors stained a rich brown. The airy twenty-foot-high foyer, anchored by a beloved antique table from France and brass pendant lighting, sets the tone for a home that is as personal as it is polished. In the living room, a pair of luxurious sofas in purple add a bold splash of colour to an otherwise neutral palette, while the custom Italian wallpaper behind the built-in bar speaks to a love of travel and art. Treasures collected across the globe, from South Africa to Morocco, decorate every nook and cranny, giving the space a soulful and comforting feeling.

This South Hill home uniquely expresses the owner's tastes and travels.

# MHOUSE INC.



FOUNDER SHIRLEY MEISELS'S unique entry into design happened organically. She initially worked for thirteen years in set and wardrobe styling before finding her way into interior design after her own home was featured in a magazine and clients started asking for her. Driven by passion and a self-taught approach, she built a sought-after boutique firm through word of mouth. Known for its personalized approach and seamless blend of elegance and comfort, Mhouse Inc. benefits from Meisels's hands-on involvement in each project, curating homes based on clients' desires and taking their vision to the next level. Drawing on her background in fashion and advertising, Meisels has a keen eye for fabrics, colour, and balance, all essential to her aesthetic. Now she mentors young designers, aiming to impart her wisdom and share lessons from her journey. This initiative, called Whouse Inc., reflects her belief in nurturing the next generation of design talent and her recognition of the challenges and triumphs that come with the craft. Meisels has appeared on *Cityline* and at the Toronto Interior Design Show as a vibrant speaker and was recently celebrated as one of Canada's Top 100 Designers by *Canadian House & Home* magazine.

Designer Shirley Meisels balances soft and hard furnishings in this bold South Hill project.

## Warm Transitional

Classic elegance prevails in this South Hill home. Meisels and her team expertly blended old-world sophistication with modern lines. When you walk into this large family home, you are greeted with a classic black-and-white marble floor, which sets the tone for what unfolds next. Black-framed windows, arched doorways, and coffered ceilings frame the perfectly proportioned rooms, evoking a European aesthetic. A dark den-office offers a luxurious retreat, while the living room and kitchen are both bright and welcoming, continuing the elegant throughline of this timeless space.

Classic materials meet modern style in this graciously sized family home.

Round contours and a natural colour palette create a sense of serenity on the second floor of this home.

The studio uses repeating geometric shapes and clever partitions in this Bayview Village home to carve out storage and privacy.

## Modern Minimalist

Drama is high in this Bayview Village home for which Mhouse Inc. conceived a bold, graphic palette that exudes big-city vibes. Artfully minimal, the use of strategic furniture pieces and artworks lends the house a gallery effect—but one with extreme comfort. In the kitchen, black cabinetry grounds the space with thin-profile shelving and brass light fixtures adding levity and elegance. The primary suite is a welcome retreat with a clever use of space, including a walk-in closet behind the headboard and frosted glass with a blurred effect in the ensuite. Throughout, bold geometric shapes are repeated along with tactile marble and warm woods for a rich, layered feel.

# Midtown Modern

Mhouse Inc. shatters convention with a sleek, daring twist on tradition in this Cedarvale renovation. Collaborating closely with architect Brenda Izen, the design team flipped an aging structure into a bold modern statement, embracing every angle with intention. Using Izen's wave-like swooping ceiling as a launching pad, Mhouse Inc. responded with interiors that complement and dramatize this truly unique space. The sunken living room is an intimate oasis, a warm family-friendly aesthetic bathed in natural light. Guests are greeted by a truly special oversized foyer that doubles as a sitting room when the large sliding doors are closed. The custom-cut marble inlay floor, repeated upstairs, grounds the space, marrying sophistication with the practicalities of daily life. A tapestry of sleek lines, warm textures, and materials, the house exudes unapologetic luxury.

The grand entryway sets the tone for the complete renovation of this mid-century home, with both the practicalities of life (putting on shoes) and socializing (greeting guests with ease) in mind.

A micro-cement finish on the range hood and a custom marble "rug" in the bathroom are two of the many special details throughout.

# ODAMI

FOUNDED BY Canadian designer Michael Fohring and Spanish architect Aránzazu González Bernardo, Odami has quickly become a standout in the design world. The couple's journey began in Austria, and after relocating to Canada, they established Odami in 2017, following the successful design of Portland Street's SARA restaurant. Their work blends Fohring's artistry-first focus with Bernardo's site-specific architectural approach, resulting in unique collaborative projects that include homes, retail spaces, and furniture. Notable projects include the Aesop Yorkville store, where Victorian influences meet modern materials, and their Pet Objects series, which reimagines household items as playful creatures. Odami's designs are deeply connected to their locations, as seen in their Rosedale project, where reclaimed wood and contemporary brickwork reflect the surrounding streetscape. Sustainability is a key focus, with materials chosen for their warmth and environmental impact. With an artistic eye, keen attention to detail, and out-of-the-box conceptual thinking, the studio has quickly become one to watch. Whether crafting a small study or a large retail experience, Fohring and Bernardo bring a refined, intelligent, and soulful touch to every project. Their work not only reflects their curiosity and drive to explore but also shows off their deep appreciation for material and context.



The studio's Clanton Park project reimagined the layout and functionality of the family home almost doubling the footprint of the original house.

# Clanton Park

This North Toronto project transformed a modest home into a spacious contemporary residence, blending traditional layouts with innovative architectural touches. With zoning restrictions preventing major exterior modifications to the height of the home, the studio instead expanded the available footprint and reconfigured the interior space into distinct yet fluid zones. The home's ground floor is segmented into formal living and dining areas, a library, and an informal family room. Wood-clad architectural "blocks" create focal points, such as a welcoming entry wrapped in oak that sets the tone for the home's interior. The extra-wide corridors are designed to be more than just walkways—Odami treated them as their own spaces, creating framed views into adjacent rooms. At the heart of this family home is a striking staircase with sharp, angular geometry balanced by a delicate curving railing. Upstairs there are two oversized bedrooms and a large principal suite, where skylights and open ceilings ensure natural light flows throughout.

Striking a balance between traditional and contemporary, this rebuild expertly combines formal spaces with flexible arrangements perfect for the modern family.

Distinct zones are created including a sunken living room and seamless doorways.

Skylights optimize natural light, funnelling it through the expertly crafted staircase.

Key elements to the redesign radically changed this Midtown home yet retained its innate charm.

## Deer Park

Last renovated in 1954, this Midtown house was quaint and well maintained but definitely of an era long past. Odami immediately saw its potential—it just needed some love. In the end, that TLC translated into a reworking of central elements, including the kitchen and connection to the garden. What was kept was the home's intrinsic charm and key historical elements. The studio reworked the side entry to enclose part of the exterior and create a modern take on a coat closet, framed by the home's original stained-glass transom. On the main floor, a once dark and segmented floor plan benefited from opening things up, ideal for the owners who love to cook and entertain. Upstairs, a large principal bedroom was converted into a home office, while the third-storey addition became a serene principal suite. A new expressive handrail runs the length of the three storeys for continuity, adding freshness to the renovated space.

# PALMERSTON DESIGN

KIRSTEN MARSHALL FOUNDED the boutique interior design firm in 2003 with an eye for crafting unique, client-focused spaces. Now a team of six, the studio has completed dozens of renovations and new builds in the city, including buzzy restaurant and retail spaces like Fat Pasha on Dupont. Marshall has also designed several of the Princess Margaret Lottery show homes to great acclaim. Steering clear of cold, hard minimalism, the studio balances warm and timeless with daring and artistic. With expertise in reorganizing floor plans for flow and envisioning how spaces will be used, Palmerston Design is able to realize homes that are perfectly suited to their clients' lives both now and in the future. Not one to shy away from bold statements, Marshall and her team use natural materials and textures to create anchor points in each project. The studio prioritizes quality and luxurious craftsmanship, collaborating with local makers and businesses on every house project.



Sculptural prominence meets natural materiality in this sitting room.

# Midtown

This project unfolds as a symphony of textures and thoughtful planning, each element harmonizing with the client's vision for a modern, inviting home. Architect Richard Librach designed the home, and Palmerston Design came on before construction to work on the interiors and plan, with the goal of creating a space that was both grand and intimate. Unique, locally crafted pieces dot the home with personality, including the dining room's brass console and lighting fixture by Toronto stalwart Commute Design Studio. The kitchen is a blend of practicality and modern elegance with a custom stainless-steel island softened by warm wooden elements and underlighting. Space for the couple's treasured antiques was also created in the kitchen so they wouldn't look out of place in this new modern shell.

Dynamic and unconventional, the bold styling of this home amplifies a robust contemporary art collection.

## Bedford

An extensive renovation masterfully balances old-world charm with sleek modernity. Inspired by London's architectural fusions, the studio's redesign plays up both the timeless beauty of the Victorian's features and leans into the modern. French doors open to the backyard, inviting natural light, while new crown moulding reinstates the home's character. Invisible hinges and recessed hardware lend a minimalist touch, allowing the original architecture to shine. The kitchen—astonishingly, IKEA—feels high-end with custom stainless legs and porcelain floors mimicking Carrara marble, a practical choice for a busy family with three children. The backsplash, a slab of Statuario marble, elevates the design further. Hidden gems abound, including a pantry under the stairs for clutter-free coffee-making and a cozy office nook perfect for homework. The exposed brick—remnants of a former porch—adds warmth and texture, while practical features like cubbies near the entrance make the space both livable and beautiful.

Warm red brick provides a stunning visual when seated at the large island in this porcelain and marble masterpiece.

## South Etobicoke

Set in South Etobicoke, this home takes full advantage of its elevated, treehouse-like setting, inviting the outdoors in at every opportunity. Designed by architect David Small, the house is tailored for an active, nature-loving couple and includes modern luxuries like an elevator for future accessibility. The centrepiece is a breathtaking floating staircase with a central spine, creating a bold statement in the open-plan layout. With a focus on nature, the home features rustic wood floors, natural stone, and custom light fixtures crafted from thin strips of wood that resemble flowers in bloom. The fixtures function as both sculpture and subtle lighting, depending on the time of day. In the kitchen, the design prioritizes family living, moving the space toward the backyard to maximize indoor–outdoor flow. Rich textures and natural elements, like stone that continues indoors from the exterior, give the home a warm, grounded feel.

Nature is on full display in this large open-plan house in Etobicoke.

## Annex

After living in a sprawling Victorian house on Huron for twenty years, the homeowners knew it was time for a change. With their kids off to university and unused rooms gathering dust, they made the bold decision to downsize to something entirely different. They found an untouched 1970s detached house around the corner. It had its own character but needed a major overhaul, and they were ready to transform it. Out went the dated brick with oozing mortar, and in came a sleek modern vision. The studio widened windows, creating floor-to-ceiling slit windows that allow space to showcase the family's art collection, and redesigned the flow by pulling the garage door forward to make room for a mudroom and powder room in the entryway. Even the original fireplace, with its signature arch, was reimagined in the same vein but with a modern twist. Every detail is thoughtfully executed, including a bold contrasting colour and material palette and graphic geometry, to craft a home that perfectly blends vintage with contemporary.

Unique and thoughtful interventions including perfectly placed windows reinvented this 1970s home.

PASTA
The Perfect Scoop
ART
ARCHITECTURE NOW!
McCall's
UMBERTO ECO
TOM ROBBINS
MC Escher
10 x 10
Frank O. Gehry

# PLANT ARCHITECT

FOUNDED IN 1994 by Chris Pommer, Lisa Rapoport, and Mary Tremain, PLANT Architect Inc. is a visionary design studio that harmoniously blends architecture and landscape architecture. With over three decades of experience, PLANT is celebrated for creating spaces that are not only functional but also profoundly attuned to their cultural and historical contexts. The multi-award-winning studio is a giant in the world of thoughtful, engaging, and poetic design. At the heart of PLANT's ethos is a deep commitment to exploration and intellectual rigour. Their design process is characterized by curiosity and debate, as each project begins with fresh research, critical analysis, and a profound respect for the unique qualities of every site. But it's not as cold and scientific as that. Their work is grounded in connecting people to place and building memories. This thoughtful approach results in designs that seamlessly connect the past, present, and future—spaces that evolve gracefully over time, remaining flexible and enduringly relevant. Whether working on expansive urban landscapes or intimate interiors, PLANT's attention to macro and micro scales is evident in every detail, from their strategic master plans to their fine craftsmanship of a single chair. With a diverse portfolio that includes commercial, institutional, residential, and civic projects, their work is guided by a commitment to sustainability, environmental stewardship, and fostering community.

PLANT Architect is known for its keen attention to detail exemplified by the repeating pops of colour and space-maximizing built-ins in this small east-end home.

## Dilworth

The renovation of this petite corner house in Broadview North was a delicate balance of functionality and creativity. With a modest budget, the studio got creative to reorient the space while preserving its quirky charm. The original entrance had been moved to the side, creating an awkward and cluttered layout. By returning it to the front of the house, a more natural flow between the kitchen, living, and dining areas emerged. Setting the tone is the whimsical exterior, where traditional shingles were reimagined in geometric patterns. Inside, the owner's love for mid-century furniture and her work as a food blogger guided the layout. A sleek, minimalist kitchen was tailored for functionality, with deep counters and custom cabinetry to accommodate both cooking and food photography. With the studio's innovative design and signature use of bold colour and unifying elements, the house now feels both cohesive and personalized.

The storied firm used traditional shingles to great effect as a textural element at the newly located front entrance.

## Airdrie

This 1940s Leaside home tells a story of thoughtful transformation. Up front, the house retained its classic Arts and Crafts character, but the rear was a different story—a sunroom addition in disrepair, a cramped kitchen, and a makeshift breakfast nook. A two-storey extension opens up the kitchen and dining areas, connecting the front of the house to the back garden. Now the star feature, the kitchen has a large central island backed by a tucked-away pantry with pocket doors to hide appliances. Upstairs, the principal bedroom was moved from the front of the house to a serene new suite at the back, complete with garden views. A glass door and the clever use of light ensure a spa-like retreat overlooking the trees. Outside, the new addition steps back, preserving the integrity of the home's façade, while inside, natural wood and bright finishes beautifully weave together old and new.

A perfectly scaled addition to this 1940s Arts and Crafts home maintains its character streetside and opens up large living spaces out back.

## Booth

A sixteen-foot-wide home was transformed into a functional and style-forward retreat merging sleek design with heritage bones. Sitting across from a park, it hides its real magic from passersby. You can't easily see the secluded rooftop deck with its modern wood stairs and industrial sheet-metal cladding. But don't let the unassuming exterior fool you—inside, it's a symphony of light, smart design, and unexpected moments. Upstairs, the principal bedroom has slim built-ins that add functionality without clutter, with a custom bench boasting hidden heating and storage that runs alongside the walk-in closet. The kitchen is a natural draw with its beer tap, wine fridge, and ample space for socializing. Guests can sit in the back, cozy by the wood stove, while still being part of the action. A playful mix of details—frosted mirrors, plate rails, porcelain tile mimicking concrete—and carefully curated collections add layers of personality to the home.

City living is maximized in an extremely narrow home. The addition plays up its form with a long, lean kitchen and sunken sitting area.

Subtly detailed modern millwork adds interest and texture to the sleek renovation.

## First

A constellation of lamps illuminates this unique Riverdale home that's part of an old dairy-processing building. The studio deftly highlighted the existing arch-topped windows, wrapping them in rich wood that carries throughout on ceilings and in the cozy office space. A glass partition on the open-riser staircase bounces light and gives the illusion of a wider space. Furniture, rugs, and commissioned artwork were carefully selected to maximize the living area for a comfortable home for two as well as a welcoming space for entertaining. The couple's eclectic art collection and travel finds are front and centre in the highly personal design. As such, the material and colour palettes were kept to a minimum with lighter wood flooring and warm white walls. In signature PLANT style, the studio has carried lines and materials from room to room, effortlessly creating continuity in look and feel.

For a couple of art lovers, the firm created an ideal backdrop with vast expanses of walls, shelving, and artfully placed lighting fixtures.

Warm wood repeats throughout the home, located in a former industrial building.

# POST ARCHITECTURE + JENNIFER KOMINEK



WHEN TWO DYNAMIC DESIGNERS sync up, the results are exceptional. Architect Gloria Apostolou, founder of Post Architecture, and interior designer Jennifer Kominek have been collaborating on high-end residential renovations for years, decades even. The friends and colleagues have a repertoire of projects that seamlessly blend architectural innovation with exquisite interior design. Their work is marked by a commitment to elevating lifestyle experiences with inspired interiors tailored to each client. Whether working on new builds or major renovations, the two align perfectly in terms of priorities, approach, and style. Both studios specialize in Toronto homes with sensitive integration of modern design and traditional contexts—the best of both worlds, as it were. Post Architecture has a long history of forward-thinking and holistic custom home designs. Kominek, too, has built up her own practice by crafting spaces with old-world style and new-world function. Together, their projects stand out for many reasons; they offer interior architecture that maximizes space and uniquely layer in artwork, rich textiles, and colour specific to each client. It's luxury highlighted by a fashion-forward approach to style that's neither trendy nor expected. From their spa-like bathrooms and boutique hotel-inspired bedrooms to boho-chic sitting rooms, the duo is making their mark on the city's design legacy.

Drama and glamour meet in this beautifully executed dining room that merges old with new.

## Borden

This Annex renovation is a harmonious dance between traditional and modern. The clients, deeply engaged in the process, sought a home where subtle elegance met innovative design. Low-level lighting casts a gentle glow, creating an intimate atmosphere, while moody pockets and hidden nooks add layers of intrigue. The heart of the home lies in its refurbished staircase—a sweet connection to the past, preserved and enhanced. The original wooden steps remain, leading gracefully to a modern ascent of glass and bronze, allowing light to flow effortlessly through the spaces. Each element of the design, from the inlay flooring to the delicate transoms and mouldings, speaks to a thoughtful blending of old and new. This artistic renovation isn't just about aesthetics; it's a personal narrative woven through every room, reflecting the clients' love for both traditional and bold, contemporary pieces, resulting in a sanctuary that is as personal as it is timeless.

Antique elements like the restored staircase and chandelier moulding create a considered connection to the past in this modern remodelling.

Drama and texture abound with brass finishes, jewel-toned tile, and luxe wallpaper.

# Amelia

This Cabbagetown renovation is a perfect example of the heritage-meets-contemporary designs that Post Architecture and Jennifer Kominek do so well. The narrow rowhouse, emblematic of the neighbourhood, has undergone a major facelift for a new century. While respecting the home's Victorian heritage, the renovation introduces modern elements that elevate and drastically improve the home for its owner. Keeping true to the era, the studio looked to Victorian commercial architecture for inspiration. The new expansive glass interventions allow light to flow deeper into the home and create a connection with the outdoors. An original newel post, a sentimental piece, has been preserved and incorporated into a newly designed open-riser staircase, marrying tradition with modern functionality. These thoughtful details extend throughout, such as the vestibule's new transparent design producing a fresh take on the Victorian era.

A modern kitchen and industrial-inspired metal doors refresh the Victorian home. The studios kept some heritage elements, including a deep clawfoot tub.

## Major

Artfully balancing the historical charm of a Victorian Annex home with modern design elements, the studios have created a space that is timeless yet distinctly contemporary. The historic brick façade, crowned with classic mouldings and intricate plasterwork, whispers stories of another era, while the bold, black-clad addition at the rear asserts a modern identity. Inside, the same is repeated—housed within the new part of the home are ultra-contemporary fittings, while the older part retains more intricate detailing. The styles meet in the kitchen in a poetic dialogue. Brass accents shimmer warmly, bridging the eras with subtle elegance. Glass plays a pivotal role, too, drawing daylight deep into the space, creating fluid connections between inside and out. Contemporary light fixtures and artwork, along with clean-lined millwork, feel at ease in their modified Victorian setting.

Heritage meets contemporary in an Annex Victorian completely overhauled to maintain its charm and contrast it with modern fixtures and millwork.

# REIGN ARCHITECTS

**FOUNDED ON THE BELIEF** that our surroundings profoundly shape our well-being, Reign Architects embraces the science of biophilic design, whereby natural elements including sunlight and organic materials, along with a connection to the world outside, are key to every design decision. Principal Jacob JeBailey believes in crafting spaces that resonate on a deep, primal level—homes that are beautiful to the eye and the soul. The studio's philosophy is not merely an aesthetic preference but a deliberate, functional approach to architecture and interior design. At Reign, biophilic design serves a critical role in fostering environments that promote calm and tranquility. JeBailey has a background in neuroscience, which greatly informs his work. The impact of the environment on well-being is something JeBailey has often found lacking in many contemporary projects, so he makes this a priority in all his, which range from private residential and mixed-use developments to urban and institutional design. Before founding Reign, JeBailey contributed at award-winning firms in Canada, Australia, and the Netherlands.

The studio found a way to include a functional island in this narrow kitchen, rounding the edges for flow.

## House Caroline

This full-gut renovation and addition for a young family turned their Leslieville house into a bright, open space that pulls nature inside. With a massive tree in the backyard as a touchpoint, the main floor now opens up to frame views of the trunk and lower branches, while on the third floor, an intimate terrace gets in touch with the treetops. Upstairs, a large skylight floods the rooms with natural light, highlighting the impressive Douglas fir beams. A fixed oculus and the A-frame style of the addition evokes a charming birdhouse. As the home is so narrow, traffic flow was carefully considered in main spaces including an ultra-slim kitchen island, a narrow staircase, and a custom curved dining bench and table. Reign blended old and new in this small space by graciously maintaining and integrating as much of the home's original façade, trim, and stained glass as possible.

Inspired by the idea of a birdhouse, the oculus window is a central element of the principal suite.

Custom furnishings optimize the seating areas of the narrow east-end home.

A warm leather banquette is a natural draw in the kitchen of this renovated High Park home.

## House High Park

Grand old Edwardian homes in High Park are always eye-catching, but inside, many of them are dark and lack good circulation and storage. This one was no exception. Reign used a large skylight over the stairwell to draw light deep into the house, instantly transforming it. From there, the studio opened up the main floor plan to allow for a wider kitchen with a casual banquette at the back of the house. A quartzite counter and a limestone finish on the vent hood add rich texture to the kitchen, which now has an easy connection to the backyard. The contrasting palette begins with the lighter-toned floors and then continues with the dark wood-stain millwork that kicks out into the adjacent family room, delineating the space but keeping it visually continuous.

## Henderson Loft

As the city densifies, finding new and creative solutions for building multi-unit dwellings becomes ever more important. Doing so with style and function was paramount to Reign's redesign of this classic Victorian single-family home. In his signature style, JeBailey uses natural light to great effect in the full-gut renovation. Under his vision, the top floors were carved up to create a double-height loft within the old structure. On the exterior, the charm of the semi-detached home remains intact and cohesive with the neighbouring houses. Blond woods and a European-style white kitchen add to the soft and serene palette. The layout of the space is key to this apartment's success; the feeling is of a purposeful loft that has none of the awkward corners or low ceilings one often finds in these retrofits. With the bedroom tucked in at the back of the house facing the yard, it is a true sanctuary in the treetops.

Rethinking the concept of a loft, the studio cleverly reinvented the top storeys of a traditional Toronto Victorian.

# REIGO & BAUER

REIGO & BAUER, FOUNDED BY Merike and Stephen Bauer in 2005, represents a bold architectural vision, marrying the avant-garde with an unwavering dedication to personal, client-centred design. Aiming to disrupt the staid and conventional, Reigo & Bauer has always pushed boundaries and redefined spaces. At the time of its inception when Toronto's residential design landscape was still caught in a sea of beige, the firm was at the forefront of introducing bold, modern finishes and artistic elements. Pioneers in a relatively conservative scene, the studio's keen focus on interior details has differentiated them from other architectural firms for years. Everything from bespoke sculptural elements to uniquely developed finishes and artistic wallpaper designs further their commitment to visually striking interiors. The studio is grounded in crafting environments that resonate deeply with those who inhabit them; their residential projects balance minimalism and intricate detail, reinterpreting traditional elements through a modern lens. Unafraid to step out of their comfort zone, they engage with their clients' needs and desires to create spaces that are not only aesthetically compelling but also deeply personal and unique.



Nothing is happenstance for this studio, which thinks through every element as it plays off the next.

## Glasgow

A meticulous transformation honours and elevates this home's mid-century elements while transforming the dark dated residence into a bright contemporary home. Originally, heavy mahogany was everywhere, from windows to cabinetry and accent walls, which overwhelmed the space. The homeowners, after living with the original interiors for a decade, sought a quieter, more refined aesthetic. To reflect this, the studio created a series of sophisticated spaces for entertaining and relaxation that graciously flow together. They worked with key existing elements such as the rough stone-clad columns that frame forest views, balancing them with modern interventions and furniture pieces. A new welded-steel staircase sets the tone upon arrival, curving up the double-height hallway to the upper floor, its slender balustrade paired with a solid-bronze handrail. Although the palette throughout the home is muted, splashes of colour are introduced in select pieces of furniture, carpeting, and styled accessories. The house is an ideal example of how the studio thoughtfully interprets the site conditions and client wishes to realize a design that's not about ego or a specific aesthetic, but rather, about crafting the most fulfilling and authentic interior possible.

A double-height stairway is defined by sculptural steel in this renovated home.

# Neville

At the base of a ravine on the east end of the city, this four-bedroom home defies the limitations of its narrow site, creating a vertical profile that echoes the towering trees surrounding it. Clad in sleek grey diamond-shaped tile, the home presents a unified sculptural form, with every gesture carefully calculated to maximize light and privacy. A bold use of simple geometries defines the structure, with triangular roof facets that slice through the air, connecting offset peaks in a dynamic dance of form and function. The south elevation's setback, highlighted in crisp white concrete boards, carves a dramatic entryway that shelters and invites. Inside, clever cut-outs and vertical windows amplify space and light, making each room feel expansive despite the compact footprint. Muted tones of green and pink subtly disrupt the serene white interiors, adding an edge that feels both contemporary and timeless.

Challenging the neighbourhood with its dramatic exterior, this home artfully pulls light into each room with cleverly placed windows throughout.

## Warren

While many might have torn down this old home, Reigo & Bauer saw its value and potential. A reimagining of the classic Forest Hill home has transformed it into a dynamic and highly livable space. Central to the renovation is the sculptural staircase, which elegantly connects the three levels with a sweeping, open design that enhances both sightlines and flow. The thoughtful removal of interior walls and reconfiguration of spaces give a sense of openness and connection. A restrained yet striking palette of whites, charcoals, and blacks, softened by natural textures like sand-coloured hardwoods and Bianco marble, establishes a sophisticated envelope for more daring furniture pieces. Subtle references to traditional architecture, such as Victorian-inspired doors and ornamental baseboards, are juxtaposed with a minimalist sensibility. Reigo & Bauer's curated furniture selection, with textured fabrics and custom pieces, further emphasizes the home's elegant interplay of contrast and colour.

The studio's expertise with geometry, balance, and scale is on full view in this Forest Hill home.

# SANSA INTERIORS

THIS YOUNG AND INSPIRING STUDIO was founded by interior designer Jude Kamal in 2020 and has quickly made a name for itself as a result of its artistic intuition and architectural vision. Growing up in a family of artists and designers in Jordan, Kamal was exposed to the world of creativity from a young age. Her passion for art evolved into a love of design when she discovered the field of environmental design at the Ontario College of Art and Design University, merging the worlds of architecture and interiors. Her journey led her down various design paths, including commercial interior design, luxury custom homes, and, ultimately, Sansa Interiors, which allows her to take on the personalized projects she enjoys most. The studio is built on creative freedom, collaboration, and a strong connection to nature. It embraces a philosophy that prioritizes holistic, biophilic design, incorporating Zen principles and modern aesthetics. Kamal's vision has attracted a team that shares her values, and she has empowered them to explore bold materials and innovative solutions in every project while staying true to their relationship with nature and their clients.

Large windows allow an abundance of natural light to flood the kitchen and dining area and provide the space with a connection to the land.

## Architectural Symphony

Collaborating closely with the owner, a structural engineer, Sansa Interiors transformed a challenging landscape into a minimalist dream that radiates simplicity and elegance. Designed to harmonize with its natural surroundings, this custom-built home follows the flow of the land, which results in a pleasing split-level layout. With a focus on Zen principles, the multi-level design connects to nature through an abundance of light, large windows, and a natural palette. In the kitchen, curved stonework and fluted wood panels took months of meticulous design and craftsmanship to execute. The open-concept living spaces are designed for family life and entertaining, with contemporary sliding doors that subtly divide spaces while maintaining a sense of openness.

Beautiful millwork is integrated throughout, adding beautiful organic textures.

## Victorian Modern Fusion

The project started in 2021, when a young couple, drawn to the character of English-style homes, sought to update their newly purchased Victorian near Roncesvalles Village. Sansa Interiors preserved original architectural elements and integrated custom crown mouldings and trim to enhance the home's traditional feel. The vision focused on maintaining the Victorian essence and upgrading it with modern luxuries. High-end finishes, including Waterworks fixtures and Sub-Zero appliances, were incorporated into the kitchen, while the staircase was rebuilt using traditional spindles. Marble slabs were selected for their rarity and timeless beauty, ensuring that the house would age gracefully. Antique pieces, such as the fireplace mantle, ceiling rosettes, candlelights, and turn-of-the-century chandeliers reinforce the aesthetic. The couple's desire for a seamless blend of practicality and style was met with a calm, soft palette, smart lighting solutions, custom-built cabinetry, and curated accents.

Original Victorian elements are preserved to capture the essence of this once rundown Victorian in the west end.

Much debate over what type of spindles to use for the balustrade resulted in a classic, simple form that doesn't overpower the space.

## Five-Tone Kitchen

Both fun and sophisticated, this five-tone kitchen was designed for a client who desired luxury finishes, an elevated cooking experience, and a wow-factor space in which to entertain. A bold departure from the ordinary, the palette is a dramatic mix of materials and textures. The focal points of the design are two contrasting natural stones—one, dark and chunky, commands attention as the island centrepiece, while the other, a light Calacatta Viola marble, brings a subtle elegance to the backdrop and range hood. While wildly different, the two stone colours and patterns are harmonized through thoughtful cabinet and lighting choices. Sansa Interiors integrated subtle tones and colours to bring the two together, including light woods, dark charcoal, and white. A sleek Zip Water system offers sparkling, hot, and cold water on demand, while the integrated cooktop seamlessly merges with the countertop. With twenty-two power outlets discreetly installed flush with the stone, the space is highly flexible in its functionality.

Seemingly disparate materials come together in a beautiful symphony in this multi-dimensional kitchen.

bauhaus

# STUDIO 1NINE1

FOUNDERS EMILIA WISNIEWSKI and Peter Kiriakopoulos harnessed their passion for interior design after first working in media. The married couple used their business acumen to launch Studio 1Nine1 from a standing start, though being naturally gifted with people adds to their skill set as designers. Holistic in its approach, the studio works on both interiors and landscapes as one, sometimes years apart as budgets necessitate. Their spaces are rife with Toronto-made furniture and products along with natural materials and plants. By working with local makers and artists, they put their energy into tailoring pieces for each client, which translates into interiors with soul and integrity, reduces shipping and off-gassing, and supports the local economy. Avoiding trends and favouring designs with longevity as well as practicality, the pair have established themselves as ones to watch.

The studio balances drama with a casual approachability, often collaborating with local craftspeople.

## Village Town

Nestled in a quaint area just steps from bustling Yonge Street, this interior design project began with a small kitchen makeover that soon blossomed into a transformative endeavour. The three-storey structure from the 1960s initially appeared stark and uninviting from the outside. Yet within, the designers created a warm, functional living space for a young, well-travelled family of three. The kitchen became the heart of their home, albeit with an unorthodox twist. Dark and moody, yet undeniably practical, the dramatic design departs from the typical white oak kitchens of the time. Instead, rich tones, custom brass accents, and integrated appliances evoke a sense of depth and refinement. The design cleverly plays with space, making the tiny kitchen feel expansive by allowing the dark walls to recede. Using scaled furniture, including a patinaed leather sofa and custom table and bench, the living area blends seamlessly. Textured wallpaper and natural area rugs add softness and personality to the overall aesthetic.

Expertly mixing materials and finishes, the studio plays with light and dark throughout.

## Family Ties

This home's transformation was nothing short of remarkable, without a single wall torn down or kitchen gutted. It was a delicate facelift—no fillers here. The challenge was turning the once-bland 1980s home into a modern social hub with soul. The living, dining, and kitchen areas needed to strike a balance between openness and intentional negative space, creating a flexible layout for a family of four who loves to entertain. Veering from a typical fireplace flanked with bookcases, the studio opted instead for a sleek stone wall and an L-shaped couch and swivel chair to encourage conversation. The project touched every part of the family's life, from the main floor to the kids' rooms and the primary bedroom, creating a space that balances style and function.

A once-bland 1980s builder-basic home gets a bold personality with a moody palette and organic materials.

## Bloorcourt

Once a traditional duplex, this west-end home is a modern take on multi-generational living. The clients, a couple who occupy the top two floors, share the home with their parents, who live on the main floor and basement. They are close while maintaining independence. Upon entering the second-floor apartment, visitors are greeted by an expansive open-concept kitchen. Originally, the staircase cut through the space, but by relocating the stairs to the wall, the studio created a layout that feels fluid and intentional. "We went a little controversial and skipped the island," says studio co-founder Emilia Wisniewski. In its stead, they opted for a custom table with an antimicrobial and fingerprint-proof Italian FENIX top. It doubles as a prep station and dining area and can easily be moved aside for larger gatherings.

Under the relocated staircase is a charming cat house with its own arched doorway.

## Roncesvalles Edwardian

Located in charming Roncesvalles Village, this Edwardian home was reimagined to meet the rhythms of a growing family. The studio designed a seamless addition, introducing a new kitchen and pantry, and a purpose-built mudroom to support the daily bustle of four young children. Warm walnut millwork on the island and framing of the doorway add warmth and continuity to the highly functional but small space. Upstairs, the children's rooms embrace a playful energy, designed to evolve as they grow. In the principal suite, the bedroom reflects the home's refined yet grounded aesthetic. Every detail, from bespoke millwork to a thoughtful floor plan, was considered to create a home that moves with its inhabitants—rooted in a sense of warmth and designed for everyday living.

Rounded edges and durable, natural materials make for an elegant and hard-working living room for a family of six.

Textured and layered in soft neutrals, the principal bedroom is a tranquil retreat.

# TARA FINGOLD INTERIORS

TARA FINGOLD ALWAYS KNEW she was destined to create—whether in fashion or interiors, her passion for design ran deep. Starting her career at Club Monaco, working on window displays and store fixtures, she found herself captivated by the artistry of visual presentation. Later, working with Calvin Klein, Fingold honed her discipline in corporate design, meticulously creating in-store visuals for major department stores. Yet she longed for more personal connections. In 1996, she shifted her focus to residential design at a time when Toronto was just beginning to embrace interior design as a luxury, and soon her client base grew. Fingold's timeless aesthetic and ease with people continue to resonate as she helps clients craft beautiful homes that tell a cohesive story that flows from room to room. Favouring spaces that are functional and built to last, the studio does not chase trends. Instead, it designs spaces that will carry people through many stages of life. Fingold's sensitivity to her surroundings guides her work. Whether designing for empty nesters downsizing or for families growing into new spaces, her keen ability to sense what's "off" helps her fine-tune homes into perfectly balanced environments that feel right in every way.

At the forefront of Toronto interior design, Tara Fingold realizes spaces that exude luxury and deliver practicality.

## Rosedale Renovation

In this stunning Rosedale renovation, the clients, who had lived in the home for years, sought a refresh that embraced their lifestyle while introducing a calming but fun atmosphere. The goal was to balance classic elegance with intriguing pieces. In the living room, softness was top of mind—curves dominate the space, from the custom seating to the unconventional tiered coffee table. Fingold created an informal yet sophisticated space, akin to the lobby of a fabulous hotel. Movable furniture and varying shapes invite conversation and relaxation, while a strategically placed mirror draws you into the deep room, creating intimacy in an expansive space. With asymmetry guiding the design, a classic Shaker kitchen is paired with brass accents and a stunning graphite and grey marble waterfall countertop. Luxury pervades in the dramatic dining room where three light fixtures and ceiling wallpaper add levity to the formal space.

A beautiful water-themed palette runs from the dining room to the kitchen.

Several conversation areas and ease of flow were top of mind when designing this long and lean living space.

This 1980s bland home was reinvigorated with Fingold's impeccable eye, merging comfort with grandeur.

## Chic Renovation Renewal

This renovation beautifully blends classic warmth with modern sophistication, creating a Manhattan-meets-farmhouse aesthetic. The 1980s home, originally lacking a formal entry, was transformed by adding a front foyer gallery and reconfiguring the interior layout to suit modern family living. Fingold collaborated with her architect husband Richard Librach to design the home, and the space is an elegant mix of city chic and inviting comfort. Wood beams and denim-stained finishes bring a cozy, lived-in vibe, especially in the kitchen, where an oval table overlooks the backyard. The adjacent butler's pantry can be opened or closed off, adding flexibility to the space. Upstairs, the principal bedroom and ensuite were extended into the attic, creating drama with high ceilings and a patinaed mirror that adds a bit of old-world charm. Even the mudroom off the garage offers a playful burst of colour, completing this stylish, family-friendly transformation.

A breezeway-inspired hallway connects the two public and private spaces of the home and exudes a farmhouse vibe.

## Envy Noir

Drama is high in this newly built Forest Hill home, from the black-and-white foyer all the way through to each room. The clients craved luxury and visual impact. The striking custom metal handrails of the staircase set the tone for each floor, while each space has a continuous feel from one room to the next. As "black tie" as the overall effect may be, the home is extremely durable and built for life with children and pets—scratch-resistant and wipeable surfaces and high-performance fabrics were top of the list. The adults have even more glamour in their principal suite, where expansive dressing rooms and luxurious showers and baths evoke Old Hollywood glamour. The office is replete with a fireplace and bar with custom metal framing. The graphic black-and-white palette is carried through to the kitchen and family rooms, where the entire back of the home opens up to the yard via large black-framed doors.

Texture and interest are created in the living area with lowered ceilings, geometric furnishings, and a custom hearth. The principal suite benefits from luxurious finishes and ample storage.

# THESE ARCHITECTS

THE LYRICS FROM David Bowie's 1995 song "Thru' These Architects Eyes" inspired the name of this studio founded by long-time friends and colleagues Colin W. Grant and Gina Schafrick. The song has served as a guiding principle, driving the duo to create architecture that not only serves its functional purpose but also elevates the human experience. Dancing on the fine line between art and architecture, they infuse every project with a lyrical essence that resonates deeply with their clients. Grant and Schafrick, who met in architecture school thirty years ago, have a wealth of experience in diverse studios and approaches. Together, they have cultivated a design philosophy that is both meticulous and expansive. They are exploring new horizons, from innovative housing solutions to mid-rise developments, always with the same dedication to creating spaces that are as meaningful as they are beautiful. Their approach is holistic, integrating every aspect of design from the inside out and the outside in. Whether in a residential dwelling, a hospitality venue, or a thoughtful community project, the studio imbues each space with a deep sense of place, responding to both the physical context and the emotional needs of their clients. As the firm continues to evolve, they remain committed to their core values of sustainability, sensitivity to site and context, and a relentless pursuit of beauty.

Architectural interiors are but one of this studio's strengths. An undulating wall both divides and connects spaces.

## House in the Hill

What began as a simple interior renovation quickly evolved into nearly a complete rebuild, preserving only part of the original foundation. The house now artfully reflects the site's natural beauty, echoing the surrounding hills. Previously, the home, which the owners had lived in for years, had started to feel cold and dated. Now the floor plan transitions seamlessly from public to private spaces, with a serpentine wall acting as a central spine that both divides and connects the different areas. The studio used a serene palette with white spaces warmed by mid-century-inspired elements, such as rich woods that draw inspiration from the home's landscape. A statement-making green staircase was inspired by the natural moss floors of the woods nearby, referencing nature in both a literal and metaphorical sense to cultivate a feeling of calm. The house offers a fresh perspective on the property, opening up previously unseen views and creating a deeply engaging, poetic space in harmony with its environment.

Responding to the site, the home follows the curves of the surrounding hills.

A ship-like quality creates drama and intrigue in the connecting spaces of this large customized home.

## House for Entertaining

This interior design project marked a significant milestone, transforming a 1980s Midtown home into a modern architectural statement. Embracing and celebrating the home's elongated lot, the long and lean design creates expansive, communal areas. Particularly designed for hosting, the first floor is anchored around a stunning Bulthaup kitchen. A floating staircase, serving as an architectural centrepiece, enhances the home's openness and allows natural light to permeate throughout. The design, which catered to the original owner, who loved to entertain, immediately won over the current residents—professionals in the hospitality industry—who cherished its sophisticated yet welcoming atmosphere. With meticulous attention to detail, from high-end finishes to a thoughtful layout, the elegant space has served as a backdrop for numerous gatherings and has been featured in multiple publications on entertaining.

This renovation was the talk of the neighbourhood, challenging the status quo and delivering a home that's as beautiful as it is practical.

## House on a Ravine

In this elegant renovation, a historic 1924 home in Deer Park emerges as a modern marvel that also preserves its original charm. What began as an interior overhaul eventually extended into the ravine behind to maximize space and embrace the natural surroundings. The studio's design carefully balances historic preservation with contemporary interventions, such as a new metal staircase illuminated by a large skylight above. A decidedly minimalist kitchen expertly mixes materials with Italian cabinetry and a stunning porcelain-clad island with extensive storage. The home's rear, reimagined with expansive windows, captures breathtaking views of the ravine, blending the indoors with the surrounding landscape. A timeless and luxurious family home, the project represents the studio's ability to reinvent a classic home with unique and contemporary designs.

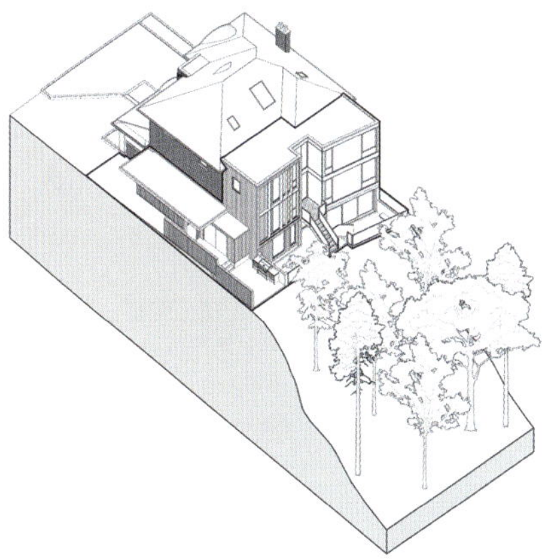

In these renderings, the Deer Park home is being masterfully reinvented, maintaining its 1924 character while bringing it into the twenty-first century with larger spaces and ample light flowing in the rear addition.

# U31



FOUNDED IN 2011 by Kelly Cray, Neil Jonsohn, and Nancy Dyson, U31 is an interior architecture and design studio that redefines the rules. Emerging from a decade of collaboration in the industry, the team has expanded from fourteen to thirty. Their expertise spans multi-family developments, luxury private residences, hospitality, and purpose-built rentals, with projects that grace the landscapes of Toronto, New York, Vancouver, and the Caribbean. Their approach is highly collaborative, with open dialogue and innovation serving as guiding principles for creating distinctive projects rich in personality and functionality. From bespoke Toronto residences to hotels in the West Indies, the firm's portfolio is as diverse as its clientele, yet the common thread remains: a commitment to elevating lifestyle experiences by designing interiors that are inspired, tailored, and diverse.

A limited, modern palette and Art Deco lines create a stunning contemporary dressing room in this custom home.

## Dream Abode

Built for long-time clients, this new build presented a unique opportunity to create a luxurious and comfortable home in harmony with the family's lifestyle. A bright and modern aesthetic was key, as were classic architectural details for character and depth. The studio achieved this balance by keeping backgrounds light and millwork tailored and simple, while introducing embellishments through custom crown plaster moulding, marble-clad columns, arched openings, graphic marble flooring, and antique brass accents. Generous volumes and soaring ceiling heights foster spacious living zones in a house that includes everything on the family's dream-home list, like a scene-setting foyer, loggia, large gym, massage room, crafts room, gourmet kitchen, bar and lounges, formal dining room, a great room, and even a hair salon.

The studio sets the tone for an instant classic residence with a stunning foyer and spiral staircase.

Meticulous planning and a keen eye for tailored functionality come together to create a house bursting with vibrant family living and unparalleled home entertaining.

## Luxury in the Sky

This ultimate bachelor pad combines luxurious finishes and furniture pieces into a modern hotel-like space. The client, a frequent traveller, wanted the design to feel tailored and sophisticated with minimal maintenance—think New York-style living. With this in mind, the design team undertook a 90 percent renovation of the penthouse, blending old and new elements, for example, retaining some original bathroom stone while introducing twelve-foot-high custom panelling and doors that required a crane for installation. Outside, a large glass-fronted, spa-like pool adds to the chic resort atmosphere on the 2,200-square-foot terrace. Inside, the home exudes warmth through architectural wood accents and high-contrast stone surfaces, all anchored by stunning chevron-patterned oak floors with a wire-brush finish. Custom furniture, carefully curated lighting, and a retractable pergola for outdoor enjoyment complete the scene for relaxing and entertaining.

Rich and timeless, the finishes in this penthouse bachelor pad offer glamour on high.

A mix of materials and cladding transforms the once-outdated space into a dynamic unit that feels like a home.

## Family Acreage

This new build caters to the client's young family and their love of entertaining. Balancing casual comfort with muted formality, the home is both cozy and elegant. Collaborating with the architect from the outset of the project allowed U31 to shape the interior's volumes. Consequently, the result is a bright, airy home with soaring ceilings and a series of welcoming and uplifting spaces. Hand-cut limestone, wide plank white-oak flooring, light lacquers, and wood ceilings create a warm neutral background, complemented by furnishings that soften and contemporize the space. The decorative lighting and fabric selections add a touch of glamour and whimsy, subtly referencing the home's bucolic surroundings and country charm. With a combination of earthy, grounding materials and an abundance of natural light, the studio has crafted a casual yet sophisticated home that will be enjoyed for generations to come.

The large living area with dramatic vaulted ceilings is ideal for entertaining large or intimate groups.

THE BOOK of SYMBOLS
Burgundy

# WANDA ELY ARCHITECT

THE STUDIO FOUNDED in 2011 by architect Wanda Ely cultivates unique residential projects that speak to each homeowner's particular story. Ely has an instinctive ability to translate people's needs and wants into something they could not have imagined—a space that surpasses those goals and at the same time is poetic in its manifestation. Shaped by years working in celebrated firms, Ely takes her architectural background and uses it to craft interiors with high-level concepts and day-to-day practicality. Taking a deep dive into the hearts of her clients, she is able to execute environments that transcend utility. Her team works collaboratively to create solutions for often challenging Toronto houses. From lifting the floor plate to create more overhead space in the basement to using nature photography as inspiration for form and colour, the studio has dozens of projects under its belt that are environmentally sensitive, foster human connection, and galvanize the use of every square inch. Each project varies based on site conditions and homeowners, giving the studio a breadth of work that is truly astounding. There is a richness and layered feeling to all their work, whether residential or commercial, that is undeniably a Wanda Ely trademark.

An eclectic mix of new, vintage, and custom pieces like the tiered coffee table create warm and approachable living spaces.

## Palmerston

Set on one of the most desirable streets in the city is this large Edwardian house completely overhauled for a busy family of five (plus dog). Ely and her team touched every corner of the house, down to designing custom furniture and selecting artwork. The main floor was reorganized slightly by removing a wall between the kitchen and den at the rear of the house. Now the large island in the chef's kitchen serves as the hub, with an adjacent lounge kitted out with an extensive built-in banquette, suspended brass bar, and doors connecting the back patio. The formal living room and dining rooms stayed in place, but were contemporized with a mix of eclectic art, furniture, and textiles. The finishes are exquisite, yet the house feels youthful and cool. Upstairs, a casual family den, offices, and tailored bedrooms exude classic charm, while the second-floor principal suite is a master class in space planning and luxury.

A classic Annex home is reinvented with a unique balance of old and new, keeping walls intact at the front of the home and opening it up at the back.

# Boston

The owners of this house came to the studio with inspiration images, which were artistic photographs of Icelandic landscapes—a poetic start to a truly unique home. Ely and her team transformed the narrow semi-detached house in Toronto's east end into a cozy and modern home with a Bauhaus feel. Riffing on those landscapes, Ely created curving millwork walls and integrated storage that evoke natural canyons and rocky cliffs. The renovation prioritized the couple's life now, focusing on creating a functional sanctuary and a dynamic office space rather than worrying about future resale value. The design incorporates Bauhaus elements, like metal tubular railings and high-contrast palettes, alongside natural forms such as a wall of Appenino marble and a curved walk-in shower. Skylights, sun tunnels, and strategic window placements flood the once dark home with light, while dramatic shadows and sculptural bookshelves add another level of movement to the unique space.

Light and shadow are maximized on the upper floor where a library, office, bedroom, and ensuite share space in this small home.

Undulating lines and unique space divisions are inspired by Icelandic photography.

## Dovercourt

This project transforms a typical west-end semi-detached home into something truly unique and personal. The owners wanted a space that reflected their family history and values. Central to the design is a cherished rice box, an heirloom from the owner's Japanese grandmother, who endured internment during World War II. Steeped in history, it became the heart of the home, surrounded by a staircase and adorned with custom screens that evoke traditional Shoji panels. The owners' affinity for mid-century modern also influenced key areas, like the dining room, where herringbone flooring creates a "floor carpet" of sorts. It's also a nod to traditional Japanese tatami mats. From the vintage lounge-inspired living room to the sunken record storage, every detail speaks to the couple's story, resulting in a modern home that is both deeply personal and highly functional.

A couple's family histories are merged in a non-traditional take on the Toronto semi.

Built-in seating dominates the front sitting room of this west-end home, which includes an integrated record-listening zone.

Creature

# WAYBACK ARCHITECTS

WAYBACK ARCHITECTS IS A GEM among architecture and design studios. The studio's work is sophisticated, and the people are as talented as they are humble. Rooted in a fifteen-year friendship between founders Stephen van der Meer and Jordan Winters, the team works collaboratively on residential and commercial spaces. Their process is refreshingly tactile, beginning each project with hand-built models and pencil sketches that emphasize context, scale, and materiality. This attention to detail is evident in their projects, where natural light flows effortlessly through spaces, and every surface and finish speaks to their commitment to quality. Whether working on laneway houses, Victorian restorations, or contemporary urban designs, the studio imbues each structure with a sense of joy and discovery. Their work balances modernist sensibilities with whimsical touches—and an element of surprise. With a passion for environmental harmony, they see architecture and interiors as one, creating homes that are steeped in the beauty of thoughtful craftsmanship.

A classic Yorkville Victorian is painstakingly restored and renewed with new furnishings and bold metal doorways.

A dark-painted hallway with classic herringbone flooring connects the kitchen to the back living space.

# Yorkville–Annex

A heritage-listed Victorian semi in Toronto's Annex was meticulously revitalized by balancing historical preservation with modern design. Outside, the home's classic red brick and gingerbread trim were restored, while the interiors were reimagined to meet the clients' contemporary needs. The studio faced the challenge of creating open, versatile spaces within the narrow older home. A rear extension on both floors allowed for lift-and-slide doors that connect indoor spaces to the backyard, while a spa-like suite on the extended third floor offers serene privacy. The heart of the home, a rebuilt staircase, acts as both a functional spine and an artistic centrepiece, filtering light from overhead skylights. The couple's eclectic art collection adds personal charm, beautifully set against gallery-white walls.

## Rosedale

In a harmonious blend of modernity and heritage, Wayback Architects masterfully renovated this Georgian-style home alongside interior designer Anne Hepfer. Originally tasked with adding two bedrooms into the attic and renovating the kitchen, Wayback's contribution quickly expanded to encompass the entire attic and a reimagining of the main floor. Drawing inspiration from the home's original oak-wrapped library, the design embodies what Winters calls "crafted modern," marked by clean lines and refined, warm details. Oak-framed thresholds, integrated closets, and sleek cove ceilings showcase the studio's thoughtful touches. Rather than creating an open floor plan, Wayback maintained a series of connected paths, preserving a sense of intimacy and an ideal flow for entertaining.

The studio modernized this Georgian-style Rosedale home with creative space planning and finishes.

Together with interior designer Anne Hepfer, Wayback finished this home to perfection with warm textures, statement materials, and artwork.

## Roncesvalles Village

A former banana-ripening and storage building sat unused behind the owner's house in Roncesvalles Village. The family asked Wayback to create a laneway-style house for them to use temporarily while they renovated their main house. After the studio radically reinvented the 770-square-foot garage and added a second storey, the now 1,450-square-foot space is a playful, modern, and highly tailored family home. It was so perfect for their life now, that they decided they would just live there permanently instead. Returning home from a trip to Palm Springs and thinking of the tropical bananas once housed here inspired the studio's colourful palette and clean mid-century aesthetic. Sneaking in an extra storey, lots of storage, and a cozy outdoor courtyard allows the space to fulfill all the needs of a busy family.

Colourful and modern, the laneway home is customized to the clients' lifestyles.

# Acknowledgements

FIRST, I'D LIKE TO THANK publisher Steve Cameron for entrusting me with this book. His creative vision, along with his professional calm and guidance, have been truly invaluable. I'd also like to thank each and every designer in this collection who let me in on their process, invited me to their shoots and studios, and gamely took on the task of sharing their life's work. After countless interviews and Zoom calls, I feel privileged to know these talented professionals. And I'd like to thank the photographers whose incredible images fill this book, and to the talented designer Paolo Ferrari for lending his voice in support of this project. This book would also not have come together without the expertise of the Figure 1 team including my wonderful editor Linda Pruessen for the poetry she brings to her craft; copy editor Stephanie Fysh, whose keen eye catches everything and makes the copy sing; proofreader Grace Yaginuma for her dedication to making this book as flawless as can be; and managing editor Lara Smith, without whom this book would not exist, for her steadfast support and encouragement. Thank you to designer Teresa Bubela, who added her artistic touch to every page and made these disparate projects come together as one. Thank you to the entire Figure 1 team, a group of professionals that I feel so fortunate to work with on everything from concept to marketing and distribution. The world needs books, beauty, art, and design. I appreciate the incredible work done to promote these talented creatives and their craft far and wide. Last but not least, thank you to my family for granting me the time, space, and support to work on this labour of love.

We acknowledge that the City of Toronto is on the traditional territory of many nations including the Mississaugas of the Credit, the Anishnaabeg, the Chippewa, the Haudenosaunee, and the Wendat Peoples and is now home to many diverse First Nations, Inuit, and Métis Peoples. We also acknowledge that Toronto is covered by Treaty 13 with the Mississaugas of the Credit.

Wayback's Roncesvalles Village project transforms an old banana-ripening building.

# Photo Credits

**ACDO** / 1–3, Scott Norsworthy; 4–7, Doublespace Photography.

**ASHLEY BOTTEN DESIGN** / 8–15, Patrick Biller.

**ASQUITH ARCHITECTURE** / 16–23, Nanne Springer.

**ATELIER SUN** / 24–31, Joel Esposito.

**BARBORA VOKAC TAYLOR ARCHITECT** / 32–37, Doublespace Photography; 38–39, Scott Norsworthy.

**BATAY-CSORBA ARCHITECTS** / 40–47, dedication page, Doublespace Photography.

**CHAPO DESIGN INC. | CHAPI CHAPO DESIGN** / 48–51, Scott Norsworthy; 52–53, Alice Gao; 54–55 (renderings), Norm Li & Associates.

**COMMON GOOD STUDIO** / 56–63, Niamh Barry.

**DART STUDIO** / 64–66, Angus Fergusson Photography, styled by Me & Mo Creative; 67–71, Niamh Barry, styled by Me & Mo Creative.

**EM DESIGN STUDIO** / iii, 72–79, Younes Bounhar, Doublespace Photography.

**GILLIAN GILLIES INTERIORS** / 80–87, Virginia Macdonald Photography.

**GREAT LAKE STUDIO** / 88–91, James Morley, Doublespace Photography; 92–93, Scott Norsworthy; 94–95, Tom Arban.

**IZEN ARCHITECTURE** / 96–101, Scott Norsworthy; 102–103, Izen Architecture.

**KIM LAMBERT DESIGN** / xvii, 104–111, Lauren Miller.

**KOHN SHNIER ARCHITECTS** / 112–115, Doublespace Photography; 116–117, Michael van Leur; 118–119, Tom Arban.

**LISA LEV DESIGN** / xviii, 120–125, Valerie Wilcox Photography; xiii, 126–127, Alex Lukey Photography.

**MHOUSE INC.** / ii, copyright page, 128–133, Kim Jeffery; 134–135, Stacey Brandford Photo.

**ODAMI** / 136–143, Doublespace Photography.

**PALMERSTON DESIGN** / 144–146, Lauren Miller; 147, Lisa Petrole; 148–151, Donna Griffith.

**PLANT ARCHITECT** / 152–159, Steven Evans.

**POST ARCHITECTURE + JENNIFER KOMINEK** / 160–163, Niamh Barry; 164, 165 (*right*), Tammick Photography; 165 (*left*), Arnaud Marthouret, Revelateur Studio; 166–167, Riley Snelling.

**REIGN ARCHITECTS** / 168–173, Riley Snelling; 174–175, James Morley, Doublespace Photography.

**REIGO & BAUER** / 176–183, Doublespace Photography.

**SANSA INTERIORS** / 184–189, Raffi Tutundjian, Jagged Lens; 190–191, Bruno Belli.

**STUDIO ININEI** / xiv, 192–199, Valerie Wilcox Photography.

**TARA FINGOLD INTERIORS** / 200–203, 206–207, Valerie Wilcox Photography; 204–205, Barry MacKenzie.

**THESE ARCHITECTS** / viii, 208–213, Scott Norsworthy; 214–215 (renderings), Soare Productions.

**U31** / 216–223, Gillian Jackson.

**WANDA ELY ARCHITECT** / vi, 224–231, 242, Scott Norsworthy.

**WAYBACK ARCHITECTS** / 232–235, 238–240, Scott Norsworthy; 236–237, Steven Evans.

Wanda Ely Architect's Dovercourt project beautifully integrates Japanese influences.

# About the Author

CATHERINE MACINTOSH is an editor and writer specializing in interior design, art, and architecture. Over the past twenty-five years, she has profiled top local and international studios as well as designers and artisans working in residential, commercial, product, and landscape design for esteemed publications. She lives in Toronto with her partner Bruce, son Malcolm, two orange cats, and one scruffy dog.